Ъ

DYEING

and

BLEACHING

NATURAL
FLY-TYING
MATERIALS

A. K. BEST

Foreword by John Gierach

LYONS & BURFORD
Publishers

Printed in the United States of America

10 9 8 7 6 5 4 3 2 1

Library of Congress Cataloging-in-Publication Data

Best, A.K., 1933–
    Dyeing and bleaching natural fly-tying materials/A.K. Best; foreword by John Gierach.
        p.   cm.
    Includes index.
    ISBN 1-55821-214-0
    1. Fly tying — Equipment and supplies. 2. Dyes and dyeing. 3. Bleaching.
I. Title.
SH451.B45   1993
688.7'912 — DC20   *93-22194*
                                                                      CIP

Photos by the author
Photography developing and enlarging: Mike's Camera, Boulder, Colorado

TO
JAN
whose love,
patience,
and
understanding
are
limitless

Contents

Foreword

I think one of the things that makes A.K. Best a great fly tyer is his conservatism. I don't mean his politics — based on many years of talk in pickup trucks, cafes, and around campfires, I'd say his political views are unpredictable, falling somewhere between those of Harry Truman and The Grateful Dead. I'm talking about his approach to craftsmanship.

For as long as I've known him, A.K. has been a working traditionalist. That is, rather than inventing a fresh fly pattern every week that incorporates the newest, flashiest material, he's spent most of his long career figuring out how to make the old patterns and styles more accurate, more durable, more effective, and/or prettier.

That's not to say he doesn't occasionally invent a pattern or substitute a synthetic material for a natural one, but he does it carefully, and only when he thinks it's a real improvement. I don't think I've ever seen A.K. try something new just for the sake of newness. He comes from that school in which you first put in whatever time it takes to fully master the traditions of the craft, and then make innovations — usually minor ones — when and if they're called for.

Part of it is as simple as using the proper proportions. If a mayfly imitated by a standard pattern has a slightly longer body and a higher wing than the standard dry-fly model, then why not tie it on a 2X long hook with oversized hen hackle wings and get a noticeably better, but still entirely recognizable, Green Drake?

If the rolled duck-flank wings on a Catskill-style pattern are too skinny when compared to the wings on the real bug, why not develop a way of using the same old material, but making the wings wider and flatter, while still stopping short of the fanwing, which is too big and too wind resistant? The result is still a Quill Gordon, but it's one of the sweetest ones you've ever seen.

There's also the matter of materials. A.K. is a stickler for quality; he buys in bulk, inspects meticulously, and rejects stuff I'd have happily bought and tied with.

"What the hell's wrong with that?" I'll ask. Turns out it's either too soft or too coarse, the barring is too wide or too narrow, there's too much web or not enough, or whatever. A.K. *is* a perfectionist, but not without reason. He understands that the best tyer in the world can't make exceptional flies out of poor materials.

And of course there's color, which is what this book is about. A.K. and I have spent hundreds of road miles around the Mountain West arguing first about the exact colors of a particular insect, and then about whether copying those colors exactly on the fly pattern makes any difference to the fish.

A.K. says it does, right down to blending your dubbing from several different colors instead of just dyeing the fur straight. "There are no solid colors in nature," he says.

That's one of the things that make A.K.'s flies so distinctive. Not only are they well made, correctly proportioned, and all look like they were stamped out of the same mold, they're also *exactly* the right color — tail, body, wings, hackle, everything. The end effect is that they somehow look slightly more right than flies by many other tyers, even if you can't quite put your finger on why.

Granted, some of A.K.'s ideas can seem a little extreme (you think, *Can details that subtle really make a difference?*) but I believe it all if only because the guy has spent a quarter of a century fishing, observing, experimenting, thinking, and tying flies professionally. Sometimes in the middle of a Blue-Winged Olive hatch on the South Platte River, with the water fuzzy with mayfly wings from the Bridge Pool clear out of sight upstream, it'll occur to me that A.K. has probably tied more than that many #18 *Baetis* patterns for sale.

And, come to think of it, I've never seen him fish an olive hatch without first catching a bug to see what color it is, just in case.

— John Gierach
Lyons, Colorado
1992

Dyeing

and

Bleaching

Introduction

This book is aimed at the average person with average income and above average interest in tying flies with the right colored materials. Large commercial materials suppliers who do their own dyeing have spent thousands of dollars on equipment and chemicals and dye their materials by the pound, not in lots of two or three necks.

The trouble is, we buy our materials one or two pieces at a time and when we do we want a specific color or tint for a few dozen flies. The large commercial suppliers simply cannot afford to offer six or eight shades of blue-dun hen necks, for example. For years I was stymied by the limited variety of colors in the materials I needed. Then one day it occurred to me that maybe I should try to learn to dye my own. If someone else could do it, why couldn't I?

I made a list of the materials and the colors of each I thought I needed and got out all my catalogs; in many cases, I could not find the colors I wanted. Then I tried visiting fly shops that offered large selections of tying materials to find out if some of the missing colors might be available from one of them. The trouble with that idea was that I like fly shops, and I spent a lot of time in each shop just looking at all the stuff, in the end usually buying something that I knew wasn't exactly right.

When I first enter a new fly shop, I usually go right to the fly bins, not only to see how well the flies are displayed (which will tell you a lot about the importance the proprietor places on fly quality and sales), but to learn something about local influences and variations. I've seen shops that sell only museum-quality flies, as well as some that sell fifth-rate rejects from the beginners' bench. The variation in quality is nothing short of mind-boggling. Most shops stock flies that are of average to good quality. Very few carry really poor quality flies, and I should point out that these businesses aren't fly shops at all. They're usually little gas-and-worm joints at the junction of a black top and a gravel road, and the owner is trying to make a buck any way he can. If that means carrying a couple dozen flies that work on the nearest creek, you can bet they'll be available at least through the summer. Generally speaking, the well-known shops carry the higher quality flies, as well as higher quality related gear of all kinds.

One thing I have noticed in all shops is the variety of colors of materials used to make the flies. You can walk into nearly any fly shop in the country and find a bin of #16 Blue-Winged Olives that have body color dubbing of at least three shades of some kind of green, and hackle and wings that range from light to dark dun. If you ask, you'll discover that in nearly every case the flies were tied by the same person. Now, most of us know there are seasonal and regional minor color variations to some of our favorite hatches. The Blue-Winged Olive is an excellent example of this because the early spring naturals produce very dark dun bodies with only traces of dark olive. As spring turns to summer, the insects' bodies gradually become lighter in body color, and then darken again as fall chills the air and water. I carry Blue-Winged Olives in two colors–dark and light–and in sizes 16, 18, 20, and 22. I'm covered for any Blue-Winged Olive hatch that may occur at any time of year. I know of only a few fly shops that consiously make the effort to stock and display two shades of Blue-Winged Olives and Olive Dun Quills in separate bins. The only obvious answer is that the fly tyer is at the mercy of whoever supplies his dyed materials.

Proportional consistency sells flies ... so does color consistency.

If you are relying on someone else for your dyed materials, you have given up a critical element of quality control, not to mention your own regional and seasonal requirements. I've talked to tyers who have said, "I can't afford the time it takes to dye my materials." I maintain that you can't afford *not* to dye all your own materials, and I have three very important reasons for that opinion:

1. *You* absolutely maintain control over the quality of the material to be dyed.
2. *You* absolutely control color consistency.
3. *You* absolutely maintain color fastness. (Have you ever noticed that your fingers sometimes change color when you work with some dyed materials? You can avoid this.)

What follows are the results of over 25 years of experimenting and keeping notes on all my dyeing and bleaching chores. All the recipes and techniques are simple enough for the average person to get good results with a minimum of equipment. Of course, this book is not going to be the last word ever written about dyeing and bleaching, but I think it will help you and provide a good start to developing your own notebook.

1

EQUIPMENT

Y̶ou don't need a degree in chemistry or the skills of a rocket scientist to bleach and/or dye your own fly-tying materials. You do need some equipment you can find at most hardware stores, and some understanding of what artists refer to as the "color wheel" (which I'll discuss in Chapter 9). The only attribute you really need is patience, and you already have plenty of that or you wouldn't be a fly fisher or a fly tyer. You simply cannot hurry the process of dyeing a $40 neck, just as you cannot hurry a drag-free float over a 20-inch brown trout. In either case, hurrying the process can only result in disaster.

If your local hardware store is well stocked, it should carry hot plates with variable heat controls. You should also be able to find some stainless-steel cooking pans there. In the professional cooking trade the pan we need is called a "half-pan," measuring 10 inches wide by four inches high by 12 ½ inches long. (An enamel cake pan will work, but the sides are not high enough and your chances of spilling the dye mixture as you agitate and turn the materials you're dyeing are nearly 100 percent.) You need the larger pan to dye large materials such as cock necks and bucktails. I can successfully dye six necks or three bucktails at a time in such a pan. Don't get any pan that is advertised as "non-sticking"; the non-stick coating on many will soon bubble loose because of the pan's direct contact with the heating coils on your hot plate.

While you're in the cooking department, get a good candy or meat thermometer so you can check the actual temperature of the dye bath. The temperature control knob on your hot plate will generally register single-digit numbers, not temperature. You should never have the dye bath temperature higher than 140 degrees Fahrenheit. (Temperatures hotter than 160 degrees will tend to curl the hackle fibers on necks and the hair on bucktails.) Find the setting on your hot plate that will give you this temperature and mark

Hot plate, dyeing pan, pie tins

it with a scratch or small piece of tape—but remember it will require a slightly higher setting to maintain a temperature of 140 degrees in a pan that contains twenty-five cups of water than it will to maintain the same temperature in a coffee carafe holding ten cups of water. Remember what I said about trying to hurry the process. A few degrees hotter might speed things up, but I know from experience that the hotter temperature will also ruin your material. And save some foil pie tins—they're terrific for holding wet materials and also help to make clean-up easier.

You'll also need good rubber gloves, a pair of tongs similar to those used in photo labs (I strongly suggest bamboo tongs, since the heat of the dye bath will often melt plastic ones, and a set of measuring spoons.

While you're still at the hardware store, get a couple of one-gallon plastic pails for soaking and de-greasing the materials you want to dye. If you don't have an extra coffee carafe similar to the kind that came with your electric coffee maker, get one of those as well—they're great for dyeing small amounts of hackle, duck breast, feathers and bundles of stripped hackle quills. Some hardware stores sell hair dryers. If yours doesn't handle them, go to the

Rubber gloves, bamboo tongs, measuring spoons, hair dryer, one-gallon plastic pails, coffee carafe

nearest discount store and buy the best commercial-grade hair dryer you can find. (Sticking to name brands is a good idea here.)

Most hardware stores sell Rit dye, but then so do many groceries, drug stores, and discount stores. Some Rit dyes are perfect for our needs and some are inadequate. The Rit colors I have found to be suitable for dyeing fly-tying materials are: #16 tan, #39 pearl grey, #15 black, #30 navy blue, #29 royal blue, #20 cocoa brown, #7 pink, #32 Kelly green, and #23 gold (for tinting other colors). Nearly all the stores that sell Rit dye carry both the standard powder dye in boxes or liquid concentrate in small plastic bottles. I'll discuss how to deal with the difference between Rit powder and liquid concentrate in Chapter 9.

High-concentrate powder dyes such as Veniard are a different matter entirely. A one-ounce container of this very powerful dye will last you several years, since so little of it is needed to achieve deep and vivid penetration. You'll need Veniard dyes for yellow, summer duck, red, orange, and any fluorescent colors. There are a few suppliers of this type of dye and there are other brand names. Make every attempt to stay with the same brand name when ordering refills, as there is variation in strength from one brand to another.

You'll need a few more odds and ends to finish out your dyeing supplies: A stack of old newspapers for pressing necks; a rack (similar to that in the photo) from which to hang dyed bucktails; white vinegar (acid fixer); Formula 409 Cleaner for spills and splashes; paper towels; a screen strainer; and a pair of lady's panty hose. No, not to wear — you, cut the legs off, sew the holes in the panty part shut, and use them to dry loose feathers after dyeing, which I discuss in Chapter 3.

You will need access to hot and cold running water, and the sink you work in ought to be stainless steel, which cleans up very easily. It's not absolutely required, but you should have some type of ventilating fan or a nearby window that can be opened to allow fumes to escape. To my knowledge, none of the fumes created by dyeing with hot water and vinegar are toxic, but you should still try not to mistake your bottle of navy blue dye for grape juice.

Drying rack, white vinegar, 409, paper towels, screen strainer, panty hose

Sink, counter, exhaust fan

2
ROOSTER
and
HEN NECKS,
SADDLES
and
BACKS

Preparing Rooster Necks and Saddles

Chicken skins, even those from the famous hackle farms, have a lot of oil in them. The trouble is you never know how much oil is present. I usually dye rooster necks six at a time; if you're going to dye more, increase the following degreasing formula in proportion or use two containers instead of one (treat saddles and backs the same as you would necks).

Carefully select your necks according to hackle size distribution and quality of individual feathers. It is very important to remember that cream-white necks, when dyed, will always give you a brighter color. Darker necks will always produce darker colors. You can only dye to a darker color than the dye natural color, never lighter. Thus your dye bath can only dye natural colors that are lighter than the dye bath. Some of the above is redundant, but I think it is very important to understand some of these hard rules before dyeing.

After selecting your six necks, make a one-gallon solution of hot tap water, $1/4$ cup of Downy liquid fabric softener and $1/8$ cup of Joy liquid dish detergent. (The traces of fabric softener that remain after rinsing seem to act as a wetting agent, and when the necks are immersed into the dye bath the dye will immediately begin to penetrate to the butts of the feathers. The dish detergent cuts and dissolves the oils present in the skin.) Combine the ingredients thoroughly and immerse all the necks at once. Stir them gently, making sure each neck is completely saturated.

One or two necks will always float to the top of the mixture. Be sure the neck at the very top is floating feather side up, as this will keep the oily skin in contact with the degreasing solution. Keep the necks in the solution for at least twenty-four hours, stirring every few hours; since the solution that is in direct contact with the skin will tend to weaken and break down as it disolves oils from the skin. Don't be afraid to allow the necks to remain in this solution for thirty-six to forty-eight hours. You need to remove as much oil as possible. I wouldn't leave the necks in the degreasing solution longer than two days, however, simply because I'm afraid the skin might begin to disintegrate, allowing a lot of feathers to loosen and fall out. But don't be alarmed if you see a few feathers fall out during this process or during actual dyeing. All necks have been scraped and stretched and handled many times before you get them, invariably producing a few loose feathers.

If your necks are very oily and you can see bits of chicken fat clinging to the skin, you can speed the degreasing process by mixing the above solution, then pouring it into your dyeing pan. Place the pan on your hot plate, set the temperature at 120 degrees Fahrenheit and add the necks. Stir frequently. The heated solution will help to liquify and disolve the thicker oils and fats. If you use this method you do not have to soak the necks for twenty-four

Degreasing necks

hours or more, as the necks will be ready for dyeing in two or three hours. When I am really cramped for time, I'll use this hot degreasing method simply because I can have dyed and drying necks in one day. The only drawback is that the dried skins tend to be a little more brittle and therefore require a little more care when tying from them.

After the necks have spent a day or two in the degreasing solution, thoroughly rinse them (one at a time), under the hottest tap water your rubber-gloved hands can stand. The hot water will help remove remaining oils. *Never* wring excess water from the necks — the skins are now soft and very delicate and will tear easily. Merely squeeze the water from them and place them on a dry paper towel or in a used (but clean) foil pie tin. They're now ready for dyeing.

Dyeing

Select the dye recipe you wish from Chapter 9 and prepare it following the instructions at the beginning of the chapter. (Double-

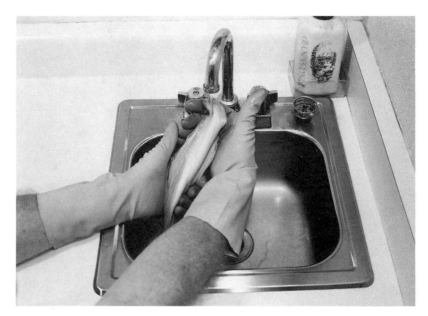

Rinsing necks

check the amounts of dye and white vinegar, and the temperature of the dye bath, *before* you immerse the necks.) Then select a couple of the large webby feathers from the butt of one of the necks and immerse them into the prepared dye bath. You will notice that the dye instantly begins to change the color of the feathers. Allow them to remain in the dye bath until they appear to be about two shades darker than the color you want. For example, if you are attempting to dye cream-white necks to medium dun, allow the test feathers to become slate dun before you remove them from the dye bath. Take a good look at this color because you need to remember how dark the feathers are at this point in the process. There are only three possibilities: They are too light, or too dark, or they're just right.

Rinse the feathers under cold tap water to further set the dye and to wash away excess dye, then rinse them again under warm (not hot) tap water to wash away any remaining excess dye. Use your hair dryer to blow-dry them by holding the butts of the

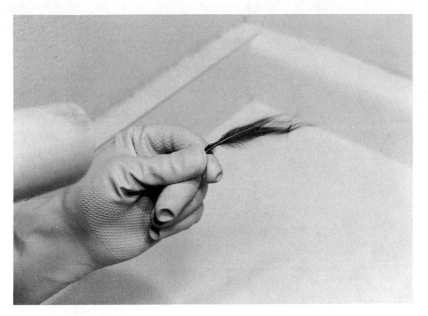

Blow drying test feathers

feathers while you direct the hot air along the quills. If what you have after drying are feathers that are too light, you should select two more butt feathers and dye them a little darker than the first two. If they are too dark, you need to remove the second pair of test feathers from the dye bath a little sooner than the first. If they are exactly what you want, try to remember what you did!

When you are satisfied that you know what you're looking for in the wet color of the dyed feathers, check the temperature of the dye bath — it should be no higher than 140 degrees Fahrenheit — and immerse all the necks at once. Gently stir and turn the necks to be certain the dye is in contact with every feather. Continue turning and stirring for the next 30 minutes because most of the strength of the dye bath will be used up during this time. If you do not constantly turn and stir each neck, some necks may absorb more dye than others; if a neck remains on the bottom longer than the others it may take on a ring pattern from the heating coils beneath the pan. The extra heat from this contact can also ruin feathers.

Necks in dye bath

When you're satisfied with the color of the necks, remove them from the dye bath — but *don't* discard the liquid yet. You may find that you'll need to put the necks back in the bath after you've rinsed and dried one, only to discover it's not as dark as you'd like. Chances are the other necks will be too light, too. Remember it will take much longer to dye six necks to the color you want than it did to dye a couple of butt feathers.

Your dye bath may begin to clear somewhat as the necks become darker, because the feathers are absorbing the dye. If, after removing the necks from the dye bath, you need to return them to get a darker color and the dye bath appears rather clear compared to its original color, add more dye to the dye bath. But you must stir it in thoroughly before you put the necks back in. You should generally only have to add one third the amount of dye that it took to make the original dye bath.

You may also notice an oily scum line around the edge of your dye pan. This is an indication that you didn't get all the oils out of

Oily scum line

the skins before you began to dye them. If there is a prominent scum line around the edge of your dye pan, the surface of the dye bath has had a very thin film of oil on it while you were dyeing your necks. Each time you turned a neck you were also applying a very thin oil film to each feather; this seems to act as a barrier against further dye penetration. This oily film is easily removed from the feathers, but first be sure that your necks are dyed at least one additional shade darker than your test butt feathers.

Rinsing

If there was no oily film around the edge of your dye pan, simply rinse each neck under cold tap water, gently and repeatedly squeezing the necks until the water runs clear. This cold rinse tends to help set or fix the dye. Squeeze the excess water from each

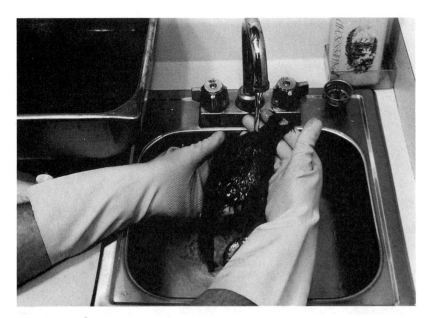

Rinsing necks

neck and, when you've rinsed them all, rinse each one again, this time under warm (not hot) tap water. The warm rinse will remove any excess dye that may be clinging to the surface of the feather fibers. Gently squeeze the excess water from each neck and place it to one side.

If there *was* an oily scum line in your dye pan, mix a mild solution of warm tap water and 1 teaspoon of Joy dish detergent. Immerse all the necks into this soapy mixture and agitate them with your hand until you are sure each neck has been in contact with the solution. (You'll notice the solution appears to take most of the dye out of your necks. Not to worry! It only removes excess dye and oil clinging to the surface of each feather and the oily skin. Remember, dye penetrates and can only be removed with a color remover or through a bleaching process.) Rinse the soap solution from each neck by gently flushing and squeezing it under warm water. If the necks are too light at this time, do not put them back in the oily dye bath. Dump the bath, clean the dye pan thoroughly, mix a new dye bath, and begin the process again. The second dye bath will produce dyed necks much faster since the necks have absorbed some dye before the oils coat the feathers. Stay nearby and check on the progress frequently.

Drying

After rinsing all the necks, squeeze additional moisture from the feathers and skins by gently rolling each neck in a folded paper towel and gently squeezing. This will reduce the time it takes to blow the feathers dry with your hair dryer.

Blotting necks

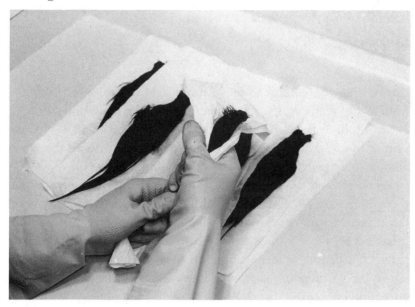

Plug in your hair dryer and turn it to high-hot. Pick up one neck and direct the hot air against the feathers as shown in the accompanying photo. Directing the hot flow of air against the natural lie of the feathers increases the efficiency of the dryer, shortening the

Blow drying necks

drying time. Be careful to move the nozzle of the dryer back and forth as the feathers dry, manipulating the neck in an undulating or vertical rolling fashion at the same time. Don't attempt to dry the skin of the neck, as it will begin to curl. Repeat with all the necks and carefully place them between layers of newspapers.

When placing the necks on layers of newspapers, be careful that the feathers are aligned and straight. Once a feather has taken a set during the drying process, it will remain in that configuration until it has been soaked, straightened and redried. A fine-tooth comb or baby's hairbrush (or even a slightly damp sponge), will work to stroke the feathers on each neck into alignment. Place three necks on a folded newspaper as shown in the following photo.

Allow the tiny tips at the bases of the necks to extend about one eighth of an inch beyond the folded edge of the papers. They will curl; when the necks are completely dry, merely break them off and trash them. These tiny feathers on the tips are usually only about one quarter of an inch long. I haven't discovered a use for them.

Necks on newspapers

When you've aligned the necks as shown and stroked all the hackle feathers into position, carefully place another folded newspaper on top of the necks by slightly sliding the top layer in the direction of the natural lie of the feathers. This will ensure the feathers will stay aligned as the necks dry. Place some weight (books work well) on top and leave it for a day. The newspapers will absorb moisture from the skin and the feathers; replace all those that have been in contact with the necks after twenty-four hours. If the necks aren't completely dry in two days, replace the second set of papers with a third set and let them cure for a third day. The amount of time it takes to completely dry your necks will depend on local humidity levels.

Storing Dyed Necks

If you have dyed and dried some rooster necks from one of the well-known hackle farms, they were probably packaged in a plastic zip-lock bag, with the neck itself stapled to a piece of white card-

Necks in shoebox

board. You don't need to re-staple the neck to the piece of cardboard, but you should carefully insert the neck back into the bag so that it rests on top of the cardboard as it did when you bought it. Then carefully place the neck in a suitable container for storage. I use plastic shoe boxes. They hold about a dozen necks and are easily labeled. The box is just wide and long enough to accept a packaged neck, yet the individual neck packages won't slide around inside the box.

Use care when handling any of your dyed or undyed necks. Try to keep them from sliding to one side of the plastic bag, as this will tend to cause the larger butt feathers to take a set. Then when you want to tie some large streamers with matched wings, you'll find that all the butt feathers may have a set in the same direction. It's just as easy to take a little extra care as it is to be careless, and it'll save you a lot of time and frustration.

Hen Necks and Backs

I don't like hen necks from the well-known hackle farms for use as winging material on dry flies. The grower's main interest in raising hackles for fly-tying is to develop roosters that have long hackle feathers with thin (but strong) quills and as many webless, stiff hackle fibers all of the same length as possible. The shorter the hackle fibers on each hackle feather, the better the quality of the entire neck.

Raising these birds involves a thorough understanding of genetics. Certain hens and roosters are kept aside as brood stock because they possess some or all of the characteristics mentioned above. So far so good. The trouble it causes for us fly tyers is that many of the hens from these hackle farms are now producing neck hackle almost as good as some of the Indian necks we used for dry flies twenty years ago! The hackle tips are too pointed and there isn't enough web to produce a suitable wing profile for dry flies. Don't get sucked into buying these necks for winging materials on dry flies just because they came from one of the famous hackle farms. (They are fine for soft hackle collars on certain wet flies, however.) A good rule to follow when buying any kind of tying material is to always open the package and examine the material carefully. If the proprietor of the store won't allow you to do that, it's usually because he already knows there's something wrong with what's in the package. You should never buy anything until you are absolutely sure that it's exactly what you want.

That said, buy domestic hen necks or pullet necks for winging dry flies. These are the necks that come from a hatchery or chicken farm that is only interested in raising chickens for egg or meat production. The hackle feathers from the necks of these hens make perfect dry-fly wings. They have well-rounded tips, each feather is nearly all web, the hackle stems are soft, there are usually plenty of feathers of all sizes on each neck, and they are far less expensive. The only drawback is that the skin side of the neck has probably only been rubbed with Borax and air-dried, and so will contain lots of fat and oils.

Comparison: genetic/domestic hen necks

Preparing Hen Necks and Backs

You will need to scrape the excess fats and oils from the skin of these necks (backs generally don't need trimming, but otherwise can be handled the same way) before you can degrease them in a soapy solution, let alone dye them. I usually first cut away the butt of the neck. This portion of the neck contains large feathers that will be of no use when tying flies for trout. I store these un-scraped pieces in a box labeled "White/Cream Hen Neck Butts." Don't throw them away, because someday you may decide to tie some large steelhead, salmon or bass flies that require a soft whispy hackle collar. This stuff is easily dyed and you usually need only a dozen or so feathers at a time. Use a single-edge razor blade (I think Gem blades are the best) to cut the skin side of the neck to remove the butt section.

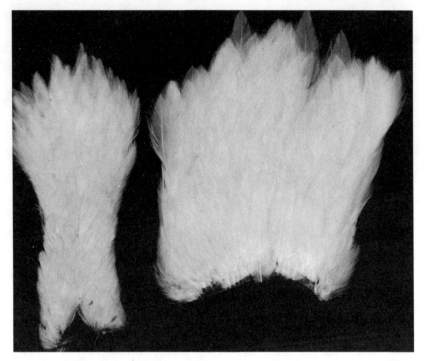

Trimmed hen neck & butt piece

Scraping seems to work best if I use an old pocketknife of the type that is usually sold as a "fish knife." This knife usually has a long, pointed blade with a slight upward curve near the point. Sharpen this blade to a fine, saw-tooth edge with either with a fine file or a rather coarse stone. The saw-tooth edge digs into the layers of fat a little easier, without tearing the skin.

Scraping knife

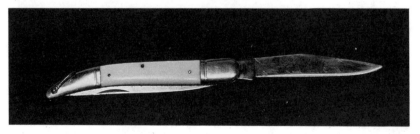

Place the neck on a piece of plywood as shown in the photo below. Then place the knife on the skin as shown in the second photo. Be certain that the knife blade is perpendicular to the skin at

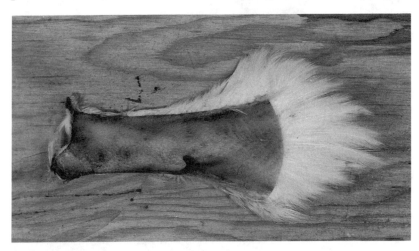

Neck on plywood

Knife in position

all times. Scrape the skin toward the trimmed butt, being careful not to apply enough pressure to tear the neck. It *is* possible to scrape the neck too thin. If you do that, most of the feathers will come out during the degreasing and dyeing processes, something that will definitely ruin your day. I can't tell you how much scraping is enough, because you can always get a little more oil from any neck by applying a little more pressure on the knife. Try to get most of the chicken fat off. When you begin to notice that all you get on the edge of the knife blade is some rather clear oil, you have probably gone deep enough. Remember, you are going to place the neck in a strong degreasing solution before you dye it.

The degreasing solution for hen necks should be a little stronger than that for rooster necks simply because hen necks are usually greasier. Use the same solution as described earlier in this chapter, but add one tablespoon of liquid Wisk. Allow the necks to degrease for no more than forty-eight hours, with occasional stirring. This solution will satisfactorily degrease ten to twelve trimmed and scraped necks.

Dyeing

Dye, rinse, dry and store hen necks in the same manner as that outlined for rooster necks. You may have to purchase some smaller plastic bags for storing your dyed hen necks. I will often store two hen necks in the same bag; if you do this, be sure to place the skin sides together, as occasionally small beads of oil will bleed from the skin as it becomes bone dry. You don't want these oils to get on the feathers of an adjoining neck. If you put a small piece of folded paper towel between the two necks, it will absorb the oils and when you pull the necks from the bag, you won't get any of the oil on your fingers.

See color plates #1, Dyed Cream/White Rooster Necks, #2, Dyed Grizzly, and #3, Dyed Cream/White Hen Necks.)

3

BODY
FEATHERS

I consider the body feathers from guinea hens, any pheasant, all ducks, chickens, grouse, partridge, and any other bird to be those feathers taken from the breast, flank, and back. They can be used in a wide variety of ways in fly-tying, from tails on streamers, wets, and dries, to dry-fly wings, wing cases on nymphs, and wings and soft hackle on wet flies. A pattern recipe will usually call for a natural feather such as partridge breast or segment of guinea feather. But a recipe may call for yellow-dyed guinea or red silver pheasant feathers — and your local fly shop has neither. It can take days or even weeks of phone calls to find a supplier who has what you need, and when you get lucky and find a source, the material is likely to be the wrong color of red, or the yellow isn't yellow at all but more of a gold. In the meantime, your once-in-a-lifetime trip to fish for forty-inch brown trout is getting closer, and the fly of choice to fool these enormous fish mush have tails of chartreuse guinea body feather segments. It doesn't happen often, but when it does, it's the most important event in your life, and you'd better dye your own. You'll have the colors you need, and there is a certain amount of personal satisfaction derived from the fact that you not only tied the fly that fooled the fish of a lifetime, but you also dyed some of the material used in the fly.

When I dye body feathers I am usually preparing materials for a specific fly pattern, so I never dye a complete skin. I merely pull enough feathers of the correct size, shape, and markings from the skin to complete the number of flies I have to tie. It's a good idea to take a few extra feathers just in case you decide you need more flies; more important, you'll have color samples the next time you need to replenish your supply of those flies. If you never tie the same pattern again, you'll just have a few dyed feathers in a bag.

Another important reason to pull the feathers from the skin is that the skins of many of the birds that provide body feathers for tying are air dried and very oily. Degreasing them is next to impossible. Many of these birds come from game farms and it's not economical for the managers or owners of these places to spend a lot of time treating the skins for fly tyers. They pick up a few bucks a year selling an incidental product from their main business, which is hunting the birds they have raised and released.

Mallard flank, teal, and guinea are usually sold loose, in bulk. Buy at least twice as much as you think you'll need, simply because when you buy these feathers in bulk amounts (say an ounce or two), you are getting feathers of all shapes, sizes, and markings. Not all will be useful. In fact, you'll probably end up throwing about half of the mallard and teal away because the feathers are normally harvested from "flight" birds. That is to say, these birds were shot out of the sky (hopefully) during their migration flights. Consider what happens to the ends of the whispy fibers on the flank feathers of a duck after it has been beating its wings on them for a thousand miles.

Flight-worn/good duck flank

Eventually, the fibers begin to break off near the tips and the result is a ragged, useless feather.

Preparing Body Feathers

When you pull body feathers from a dried skin, be careful to clip off any tiny pieces of skin that stay attached to the butts of the feathers. This skin is mostly fat and oil and when it gets in the hot dye bath the oil will ruin your feathers. Feathers purchased in bulk normally don't have this problem, but you'd be wise to inspect them anyway (and clip the butts off any feathers that may have bits of skin clinging to them.)

Measure one tablespoon of Joy and one tablespoon of Downy fabric softener into an empty one-gallon plastic container, then fill the container to within two inches of the top with hot tap water. Stir to make sure all ingredients are thoroughly mixed. Add the feathers you are going to dye and stir them in well to make sure each feather is thoroughly saturated. The above solution will degrease about three large handfuls of mallard flank feathers. An overnight soaking is usually enough to degrease most body feathers; it's a good idea to stir them before going to bed.

After the feathers have soaked, place a screen strainer in your sink and pour the feathers and soapy solution into the strainer. Run lukewarm water over the feathers to rinse away most of the solution; it helps to gather the feathers in your hands and gently squeeze and release several times as you rinse. When you're satisfied that the feathers have been well rinsed, squeeze as much water from them as possible and place them in a pie tin or on a paper towel.

Dyeing

I dye almost all my loose body feathers in a coffee carafe of the type that comes with a standard automatic drip coffee maker. These carafes normally hold about twelve cups of liquid, a capacity I have found adequate. Not only is it an easy item to work with because it has a handle, but since it's made of glass I can see into it and have a pretty good idea of how well the dyeing is progressing. It's also much easier to pour out the entire mix into the screen strainer when I have reached the color I want.

Select a recipe from those listed in Chapter 9. Keep in mind that we're using a twelve-cup container for the dye bath, so you should only need one tablespoon of liquid working solution of Rit dye or one quarter teaspoon of powdered concentrated dye. Put about ten cups of hot water into the carafe, place it on your hot plate and adjust the heat to a setting that will produce a temperature of 140 degrees Fahrenheit. Add the dye and about two tablespoons of white vinegar, mix well and test dye a single feather to determine your dye bath is the proper strength. When you are satisfied that the dye bath is correct, add the feathers all at once. Stir to make sure the dye comes in contact with each feather.

Always remember that the color of wet material will appear to be much darker than it is when it is dry. When you think you're getting close to the desired color, remove one feather from the dye bath and rinse it, first under cold water to set the dye, then under hot water to remove any excess dye. Squeeze the feather in a paper towel and then use a blow dryer to completely dry the feather. You'll know in just a few minutes if you have reached the color you're seeking. If the feather is too light (which is usually the case the first time you try this), return it to the dye bath and allow the dye to work a little longer. If you have reached the desired color, immediately dump the dye bath and feathers into the screen strainer and thoroughly rinse in cold water, then hot. Put your rubber gloves on and squeeze and release the ball of feathers as the hot water runs over them to make sure that you are washing away as much excess dye as possible.

Drying

Roll the ball of feathers in a couple of sheets of paper towel and squeeze firmly to remove as much moisture as possible. Remove the paper towels, place the ball of feathers in your screen strainer and cover the top with the panty part of a pair of panty hose. (To prepare this vital piece of equipment, simply cut the legs off a pair of panty hose and sew the leg holes shut. The elastic waistband will stretch nicely around the top of the screen strainer, creating a bag that will hold the feathers.)

Hold the strainer as shown in the photo on the following page and direct the air from the hair dryer (set at high-hot) onto the feathers while gently shaking the strainer. In just a few minutes some of the feathers will begin to bounce around in the panty-hose bag. Now raise the strainer so that you're directing air into it as shown in the photo on the following page.

When you think the feathers are dry enough, empty them onto a couple of layers of newspaper in a place away from drafts from

Panty hose

Panty on strainer

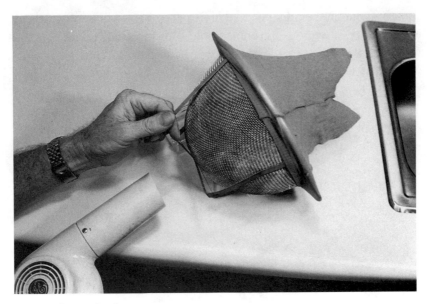

Drying loose feathers

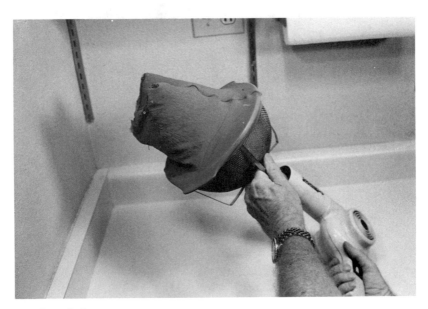

Air from below

nearby windows or doors; a sudden gust of air will send feathers flying all over your workroom. Some moisture will remain in the stems of the individual feathers after blow drying. To prevent mildew, which might occur if you immediately seal the feathers in a zip-lock bag, give them some time to air dry. I usually leave mine on the newspapers overnight before storing them in an air-tight bag.

See color plates #4, Natural and Dyed Mallard Flank, and #5, Dyed Silver Pheasant.

Loose drying feathers

4

BUCKTAILS

First and foremost, always try to get skinned and bleached bucktails. They are a lot easier to work with and are well worth the small additional expense — and they smell a lot better. But even if your supplier lists his skinned bucktails as "bleached white," nearly all will still smell rather strong. I always soak and degrease all my bucktails even if I'm not going to dye all of them. Your tying room will smell better and so will you and your flies.

I'm sure most of you noticed long ago that not all bucktails are the same. In case you haven't, there are a few things to consider before selecting bucktails for dyeing. Some have long and rather straight hair, while others have short and wavy hair. Some have light tan backs; some have nearly black backs with only the slighest brown marking. I like to select the lightest color back (light tan) for dyeing to yellow, red, green, or blue because often the color I get on the back of the dyed bucktail can be useful in some other tying project. Save the dark-backed bucktails for dyeing to brown, black, or navy blue.

Consider tying needs other than color, as well. For example, if you're going to be tying Mickey Finns, you won't need to dye bucktails that have mostly three to four-inch hair. You'll be throwing away roughly an inch and a half of hair every time you tie in a clump of bucktail. Save the long-haired bucktails for large saltwater flies or bass bugs. If you want your flies to look bulky without actually having a lot of hair in them, dye the wavy-haired bucktails. If you want your flies to have a slimmer profile, dye the bucktails with straight hair. If you don't spend a few minutes thinking about this before you start dyeing, you'll soon sit down to tie and discover you have the wrong kind of hair to work with.

Some bucktails have excess body hair and fat on the skin near the butt of the tail. I will often cut off the last two inches or more of the butt, since this hair is hollow and very bulky. It flares when tied in and thus isn't suitable for streamers. However, if you want to gradually build up a supply of dyed hair for spinning bass bugs, leave it attached. Make sure you scrape off as much of the dried body fat from this area of the bucktail as possible and, after you have dyed and dried the bucktail, break off the last two inches of the butt and throw it in a box labeled "Dyed Deer Hair for Spinning."

When I dye bucktails I always try to wait until I need to dye more than just one color. I can degrease several bucktails at once and thereby save some extra time. A large bucktail contains a lot of surface area, considering all the individual hairs on one, so I never dye more than three at a time in the same dye bath. This gives me more control over the dyeing of each bucktail, as well as more consistent color from one dye session to the next. If you think you only need to dye one yellow bucktail, you'd be far better off if you dyed two or three, giving you several bucktails that are all the same shade of yellow.

Regular and long bucktail

Degreasing Bucktails

In a bucket mix three gallons of hot tap water, one quarter cup of Downy fabric softener, one quarter cup of Wisk liquid laundry soap, and one fourth cup of Joy dishwashing liquid. That's a lot of soap, but it has to degrease what is often some very oily and greasy material without your having to resort to commercial-grade degreasers. Allow the bucktails to soak for at least twenty-four hours in this solution before attempting to dye them. Two days is better.

Before you begin dyeing, rinse each bucktail under lukewarm tap water, repeatedly (and gently) squeezing and releasing the tail in your hands. Don't twist or wring the tail; the skin becomes quite soft and will tear very easily. Place the rinsed tails in an empty pie tin and, when you have rinsed them all, discard the degreasing solution and perform any necessary clean-up before dyeing.

Dyeing Bucktails

Select a dyeing recipe from those listed in Chapter 9. I usually increase the strength of the recipe twenty-five percent for bucktails (again, because of the large surface to be dyed). Generally, this is a fairly simple calculation, since most of the time you will be dyeing bucktails to some common primary color such as yellow, red, or blue. After some experience with dyeing all materials, you will soon discover how to "fudge" recipes to achieve different tints. Always write down your successes so you can duplicate the results.

If the recipe calls for a mixture of dyes or a single solid-color dye, I use a single-edge razor blade to slice off a small section of the white hairs near the butt of the bucktail and test dye it, as I do with other materials. It adds a little extra time, but can save hours of time, and bucktails, if the recipe needs adjusting before I throw several bucktails in the dye bath.

When you are satisfied with the strength of the dye bath, immerse all the bucktails at once, immediately stirring and agitating them in the dye bath. During the first few minutes of dyeing, the dye mixture must penetrate right down to the skin. It will take a little longer to achieve the color you want, since many of the hairs on a bucktail are much harder than feathers, and therefore do not absorb dye as rapidly. (I can't tell you how long this might take. Just make sure you have a couple of hours to spend before you begin.) Again, the color of the bucktails in the dye bath will appear to be much darker than after rinsing and drying. You may discover that the white hair near the butt of the tail takes a little longer to dye than the white hair near the tip. When you lift an individual tail to inspect its progress, always check both ends, keeping in mind that as the dye drains from the butt of the tail toward the tip, the tip will always appear darker simply because it holds the liquid longer. Put your rubber gloves on, pick up one bucktail, hold it over the dye bath and gently squeeze the dye out of the entire tail so you can get a better idea of what's happening.

If the dye bath starts to clear and your bucktails aren't dark enough, add some more dye to the dye bath — as long as you're not using a mixture of dyes. For example, if you're dyeing bucktails to yellow, you can merely add more yellow to the dye bath. If you are dyeing bucktails to a dirty blue dun in a dye bath that contains both tan and gray dyes, dump the weakened solution and mix another batch. When you add dye to a weakened solution of mixed dyes, the color of the added dye mix usually changes. The color of the dyed material is never what you think it's going to be. Then again, you might discover something.

Always remove the bucktails from the dye bath before adding more dye, and be certain that the added dye is completely dissolved and mixed before putting the bucktails back in.

Rinsing and Drying

When you are sure that all the bucktails in the dye bath are at least two shades darker than the color you want, remove them and rinse them under cold tap water, gently squeezing and releasing until the cold water runs clear. (Don't dump the dye bath yet!) Then adjust the tap water to hot and repeat the rinsing process with each bucktail. You will notice a lot of excess dye being washed away as you do this. Don't be alarmed. You are merely washing away loose dye particles clinging to the hairs that would otherwise come off on your fingers as you tie. To further ensure that you have removed all the excess dye from the bucktails, mix a weak soapy solution of two gallons of lukewarm tap water and one teaspoon of Joy. Immerse the bucktails and gently squeeze and release them while they are immersed. This will release even more dye. You're not taking any color out of the hair, merely removing loose dye that clings to the outside of the hair and skin. Oils that were present in the skin, even after degreasing, will cook out during the dyeing process and cause some dye particles to cling to all the bucktails' surfaces.

Rinse the bucktails one at a time under lukewarm tap water to remove the soapy solution and loose dye, then squeeze as much water from them as possible. Place one bucktail on two layers of

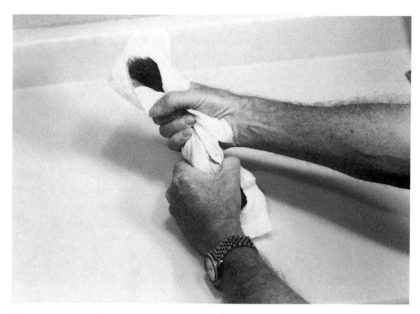

Blotting bucktail in paper towel

paper towel, roll it up from the sides and squeeze to blot away more water.

Turn your hair dryer to hot-high and direct the blast of air against the natural lie of the hair while gently rolling the bucktail from butt to tip. As the hair dries you'll discover how well the dyeing worked. See photo on following page.

(The first time I dyed bucktails, I had to start over at this point because I discovered when they dried that they weren't nearly as dark as I thought they would be. Now you know why I said a little earlier, "Don't dump the dye bath yet!" This is one of those slightly aggravating situations that you have to chalk up to experience. The next time you dye bucktails you'll be able to make the judgment of when they're dark enough with far greater accuracy. If your bucktails are too light, put them back in the dye bath and give them some more time. If the dye bath has weakened, either add more dye or mix a new solution.)

Use the hair dryer on the bucktails until the hair feels dry to the touch. Use a comb or hair brush to align the hair naturally and then

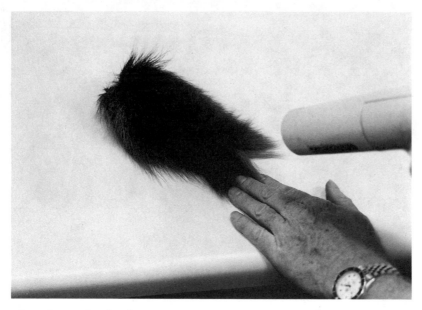

Blow drying bucktail

hang the bucktails by their butts to air dry the skins. I haven't found it necessary to place bucktails between layers of newspaper to prevent curling of the drying skins. Sometimes there will be a slight curl and this can be detected before the skins are truly dry. I press *these* bucktails between layers of newspaper to make sure the skins stay straight as they become bone dry. An arrow-straight bucktail is much easier to work from than one that has curled, and it's much easier to store.

I made a simple drying bar for bucktails, calftails, and squirrel tails by taking a four-foot piece of one-inch-square pine and attaching screw hooks at three-inch intervals. I use plastic-coated wire spring clips to hold the tails, hanging them from the drying bar by putting one of the loops of the spring clip over the open screw hook. I use a small C-clamp to hold one end of the bar to a shelf in my dyeing room. The bar is close to the wall and out of the way when in use and when I don't need it I can easily remove it and stand it in a corner.

After the bucktails are completely dry you should take a little

Drying bar & bucktails

care storing them to prevent some of the hair from taking a set. I don't use plastic bags to store individual bucktails, because it's expensive and wastes time. Plastic shoe boxes stack nicely, are easily labeled with tape and a magic marker, and are long enough for all but giant bucktails. If a bucktail is too long to fit in your shoe box without curling the hair at the tip of the tail, cut or break it in half. You'll find the shorter piece easier to work with anyway. When you place the bucktails in the shoe box, be sure that all the hairs are laying naturally and carefully place the shoe box where it won't be bumped or forgotten. A sudden bump will cause bucktail to slide against one side of the box; the hairs that are pressed against the side will take a set in only a few days time.

(See color plate #6, Dyed Bucktails.)

5

DEER
and
ELK BODY
HAIR

T ry to get your deer and elk body hair in chunks that are about ten or twelve inches square. This might be a little hard to do if you happen to live in an area that has only a few small fly shops or where deer and elk hunting are not popular. Someone has to cut a full hide into those little two-inch patches that we find in our fly shops, and it might as well be you doing the cutting because you can cut the hide to any size you want. The trouble with those little square patches is that they're very difficult to work with, especially after they've been dyed. They are as hard as little flat bricks. I think it's far easier to work from a ten-inch strip of hide that is only three quarters of an inch wide. The narrow strips are a lot easier to dye, since more hair is exposed on the side.

If you live in an area with good deer or elk hunting, you can probably find someone who hates to throw away the hides. Develop a close and lasting friendship with this person. I don't know how you're supposed to skin a deer or an elk, but I think I could do it if I had to. What I *do* know how to do is cure the hide. I don't mean tanning, or curing, with fancy powerful chemicals. I mix a pound of cheap salt and a pound of borax and spread the mixture a quarter-inch-thick on the skin side of a scraped and stretched hide.

You can make your own stretching rack if you think you really want to get into hide curing. I made one from 1"×4" pine boards seven feet long. It was rectangular in shape and one end of the rectangle was left unassembled. The closed end was held together with only a single quarter-inch bolt and nut on each corner. This allowed the side arms to swing out for stretching. I could than attach the bottom of the rectangle to the sides by another quarter-inch bolt and nut at any point I chose. Then I drilled several holes in both the top and bottom boards, one inch apart, to allow for different size hides as well as to adjust as the hide cured.

After you have tacked the hide to the frame (I use shingle nails because they don't get rusty), turn it upside down (hair side up), lay the assembly on your driveway and hose the hair side to wash away all the accumulated dust and dirt. Make sure you direct the stream of water with the natural lie of the hair. Stand the frame up and shake it to remove the excess water and scrape away as much of the body fat clinging to the hide as possible.

When you're satisfied the hide is clean, select a space large enough to store this assembly in a nearly horizontal position. Brush the hair side with a sparse, coarse-bristled brush to align the body hair. Turn the assembly over and apply a layer of salt and borax about a quarter-inch thick over the entire skin side of the hide. Raise the head end two or three feet to encourage drainage of excess liquids and try not to bump it for the next three or four days.

You may find that in as little as one day the hide appears to be a little limp. Adjust the sides and bottom of the rack to take up the slack. Remember that the more you stretch the hide, the thinner and more flexible the skin will be when it's dry. You'll know when the skin has completely dried because the salt and Borax mixture will start to loosen. Depending on your local humidity level, complete drying could be as little as three or four days or as long as a couple of weeks. The skin beneath the salt and borax will be a whitish color and will feel dry and rather stiff to the touch as it dries. Use a trowel or small scoop to remove as much of the salt and borax as possible. (Save it for use on the next hide.) Then brush the remaining salt and borax particles from the skin with a stiff brush.

Remove the skin from the rack and cut it in pieces ten or twelve inches square. Make the first cut down the center of the back and then use a marking pen and a yardstick to measure out a grid of ten, or twelve-inch squares. Always cut from the skin side. I like to use an adjustable matte knife for this procedure because the blade can be adjusted for depth of cut and I'm not cutting through lots of good body hair each time I cut another piece. Throw away the trims near the edges where you tacked the hide to the drying frame.

Carefully store the large chunks of hair in a box big enough to accept them without curling the hair on the ends. If you live in an area where moths hang out, throw a dozen moth balls in each box, tape the box tightly and store it in a dry spot. You will have enough deer hair for many years of fly-tying. You might even have some material for barter if you did a good job of treating the hair side so that the hair is straight and clean. A couple dozen Muddlers or hoppers to the hunter who donated the hide will absolutely guarantee that you'll get another any time you want it.

Selection

Be careful about your selection of pieces to be dyed. Dark hair will only produce darker colors than the original natural color. Bright yellows and clear fluorescent colors can only be produced from *white* hair. Use lighter-colored flank hair to get reds, olives, and dark blues. Use the darker hair from the back areas for dyeing to browns and blacks. You can dye directly to black if you use the darkest hair on the skin. You should usually dye any material to red or brown before attempting to achieve a good coal black, but in this case, where some hair will naturally be deep brown, it isn't necessary. A good rule of thumb to follow when selecting any material to dye is: "You must have white to dye to bright."

Degreasing

If you're going to dye air-dried or tanned deer or elk, first cut the piece into three-quarter-inch wide strips. Tanned deer and elk need no degreasing since the tanning process removed all the natural oils and fats from both the hide and the hair. Tanned elk or deer do need to be readied for dyeing with a couple of hours of soaking in a one-gallon mixture of hot tap water and a cap full of Downy fabric

Ten inch × 3/4-inch deer body strip

softener. This will soften the hairs, allowing them to accept the dye more quickly and absorb it more deeply. The small amount of fabric softener that may remain after rinsing seems to act as a wetting agent for the dye. Simply rinse each piece thoroughly before putting it in the dye bath.

Air-dried elk and deer need to be degreased. Use the same formula as outlined for degreasing bucktails.

Dyeing

Select a color from the chapter on dyeing recipes, mix the dye bath thoroughly, add white vinegar for fixative and test dye a small piece before you add the entire batch of deer or elk pieces. The recipe you choose may need some alteration to achieve the color you want. Again, the color you get from the dye recipe will depend on the natural color of the material you start with. When you are satisfied that you have a recipe that will produce the color you want, add all the pieces to be dyed at the same time. Use tongs or your hands (put on your rubber gloves) to work the dye into the center of each piece to make sure that the dye is penetrating right down to the skin. Agitation and stirring are very important during the early stages, since this is when the dye is at its greatest strength.

Again, it is important to remember that the pieces will appear much darker while they are in the dye bath than after they have been rinsed and dried. Trial and error are great teachers. When you think the pieces have reached the color you want, rinse one piece, blot with paper towels, and use the hair dryer to dry the hair. You'll know in just a few minutes if you have achieved the color you want. If you have, remove all the pieces and rinse under cold water to set the dye. Mix one teaspoon Joy liquid into one gallon of warm water and immerse all the rinsed pieces. Swirl them around with your tongs and gently squeeze and release each piece to flush out as much excess dye as possible. It'll look as if you're washing out all the dye, but again, you're only washing out the dye that would come off on your fingers as you tie with this material later. Rinse the pieces under lukewarm tap water until the water runs clear. Squeeze the excess water from each piece, roll them in paper towels and squeeze again to blot away as much moisture as possible. Do not wring or twist the pieces or you will surely tear the soft skin.

Drying

Dry the hair by directing the hot flow of air from the hair dryer against the natural lie of the hair. When the hair is dry, place each piece on several folded newspapers and stroke the hairs into alignment with a soft-bristled brush or comb. Carefully place another layer of folded newspapers on top of all the dried pieces and place to one side. Put some weight on top of this stack to make certain there is no curling of the skin as the pieces dry. Replace wet papers with fresh dry papers after about half a day. The newspaper layers absorb the moisture from the damp skin and you should have dry pieces in just a couple of days.

1. *Cream/white rooster neck ringed with all dyed colors*

2. *Grizzly rooster neck ringed with all dyed colors*

3. *Cream/white hen neck ringed with dyed colors*

4. *Natural mallard and mallard dyed to wood duck*

5. *Natural silver pheasant and silver pheasant dyed to red*

6. *Dyed bucktails*

7. *Dyed calf tails*

8. *Bleached deer, moose, peccary, grizzly rooster & hen necks, brown rooster neck, fox squirrel tail, mink tail*

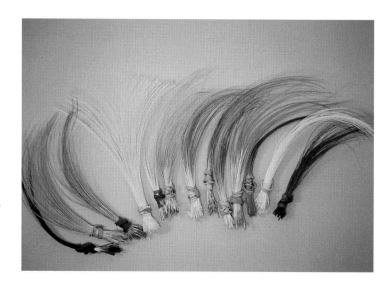

9. *Stripped & dyed rooster hackle quills*

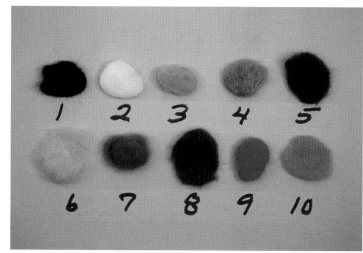

10. *Base colors of dubbing furs*

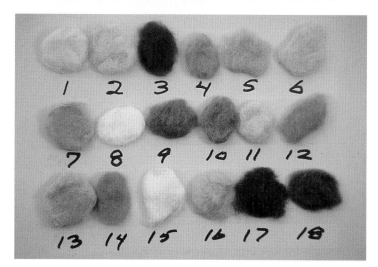

11. *Dubbing blends*

6

SQUIRREL
and
CALF
TAILS

Both squirrel and white calf tails are frequently air dried with the bone left in. You will occasionally be able to find skinned calf tails, but they too will be air dried. Both squirrel and calf tails, whether skinned or not, need to be degreased for at least twenty-four hours for squirrel and thirty-six to forty-eight hours for calf tail. The hair on both is very hard and the dried skins contain some dried flesh and fats. Calf tails contain a lot more of both simply because they have a greater diameter.

You need to be selective when you choose calf tails to dye because, as with bucktails, not all are alike. Some have hair that is fairly straight and long that you might want to use on large fresh-water streamers or bonefish flies. This type of calf tail often has hair that is similar in texture and appearance to polar bear. Others have hair that is rather short and very curly. Save these for winging Royal Wulffs or for use as parachute wing posts, or down hair-wings on Trude patterns. If I have several calf tails that have extremely long and rather straight hair, I will save them for streamer hair-wings on flies such as the Black Nose Dace. The trouble is, these exceptional calf tails look very nice when dyed and seem to have even more sheen. They make exceptionally fine Mickey Finns, for example. I'd advise you to buy any calf tail you can find that has that polar-bear quality to it and very little black hair near the base of the tail.

Selecting squirrel tails is somewhat simpler in that you will usually only be dyeing those from gray squirrels. The only time I have ever dyed a fox squirrel tail was when I needed some black squirrel and didn't have any. Fox squirrel dyes to a very nice black and seems to have a little more shine to it than does natural black squirrel or black bear body hair. Select the tails to be dyed by first taking

Short-long-hair calf tails; well-marked & dark gray squirrel tails

note of the length of the hairs. Some gray squirrel tails are very well marked with black and white barring and others are not. Some have very long hair and others have very short hair. My favorite gray squirrel tail to dye is one that has very long hair beginning near the base of the tail as well as prominent black and white barring. If you are contemplating dyeing a gray squirrel tail that has a grayish band rather than white, you won't get the brilliant yellow or lime green that is so often needed in many saltwater patterns. The same rule applies here as with dying deer and elk body hair. "You must have white to dye to bright."

Degreasing

Mix a solution of one cap full of Downy liquid and one tablespoon of Joy in a one-gallon plastic container nearly full of hot tap water. Immerse the tails (calf or squirrel) butts down and try to remember to stir them occasionally. Allow them to soak for at least twenty-four hours for squirrel and thirty-six to forty-eight hours for calf. The above solution will degrease up to a dozen tails at a time.

Dyeing

Select a dyeing recipe from Chapter 9, mix up the dye bath, add the white vinegar for fixing and then break or cut off a small section of the butt of one tail. Use this short section as a test piece to determine if you have mixed your dye bath in sufficient strength or in the correct proportions. The time to make any alterations to the recipe is before you dump all the calf or squirrel tails into the dye. (If your calf tail has a one- or two-inch section of naturally black hair near the butt, cut it off and either throw it away or keep it for later use. I've never found a use for this short black hair, however.) It will take a little longer than you might imagine to achieve a good solid color on either calf or squirrel tails. The hair on both is very dense and rather hard. Neither seems to want to take a dye easily. Don't make a common mistake of increasing the strength of the dye bath simply because it seems to be taking much longer to dye these tails than it did to dye hen necks, for example. It is possible to have your dye bath too strong, and the result will be a deeper or darker color than you thought you would get. For example, if your yellow dye bath is mixed too strong, the white material you are attempting to dye will soon begin to take on a slight orange tint. Once calf tail or squirrel tail has accepted a dye, it is very difficult to remove it. (We'll get into removing dye later.) Also, don't make another common error of cranking up the temperature setting of your hot plate in an attempt to speed up the process. You'll probably ruin every hair on the tails. Agitate and stir the tails in the dye bath about every five minutes to ensure that there is active dye in contact with all the hairs on each tail.

Remove one tail from the dye bath when you think it's reached the proper color and rinse it under cold tap water to set the dye, then rinse under hot tap water to remove excess dye. Gently squeeze and release as the water flows over the tail. When the water runs clear, squeeze most of the water from the tail but do not wring or twist the tail as this will pull the hair out of the skin. Roll the tail in a couple layers of paper towel and squeeze again to blot away as much excess moisture as possible.

Drying

Lay the tail on a clean work surface and (holding the tail by its tip with one hand) direct the hot air from your blow dryer against the natural lie of the hair. This allows the blast of hot air to penetrate down to the skin and dry the hair much faster.

You'll know in just a few minutes if you have dyed the tails long enough. I very seldom get it perfect the first time. The dry hair is *much* lighter in color than it is when it is wet. Since there isn't

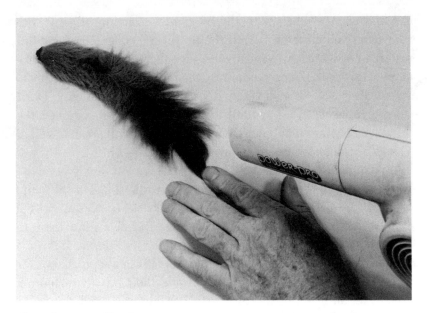

Blow drying calf tails

nearly the amount of surface area to be dyed with calf or squirrel tails as there is with bucktails, you shouldn't have to add more dye to the dye bath if your dried tail appears to be too light. It only means that you have now learned how hard the hair on a calf tail or squirrel tail really is and that it really does take longer to dye them. If the dried tail is too light, just put it back in the dye bath and give the whole batch a little more time. "A little more time" could be as much as an hour or as little as fifteen minutes. Your patience and desire for true color will govern how much time is "a little more time."

When the tails really have reached the color you want, remove them from the dye all at the same time and rinse under cold and then hot tap water as described above. Squeeze and blot with paper towels and use the hair dryer to dry the hair as described above as well. Use the same technique for either calf or squirrel tails.

Earlier, I described a drying bar I made for hanging bucktails for drying. Use the same technique to complete the drying process for calf and squirrel tails. Hang one calf tail or squirrel tail from a wire clip and align the hair naturally by gently encircling the tail with your hand and stroking toward the tip several times. (Pressing this material between newspapers will cause the hair to bend and take an unnatural set.) Hang the tails by the butts as shown in the photo below. They will be completely dry in only a couple of days. Don't store them away in a box until they are bone dry. Remember, the dried tails contain bone, flesh, and tendons that will create a hell of a smell if you allow any mold or mildew to grow on them. You will be able to determine how well they are drying by trying to bend the tail. If the tail bends easily and seems rather flexible, it's still quite damp. If the tail seems rather stiff or breaks easily (as squirrel tail often does), it's dry and ready for storage. I always allow them to hang for an extra day or two just to be on the safe side.

I like to store my dyed calf and squirrel tails in a separate box for each color. If space is a problem for you, then I'd advise putting each dyed tail in a long narrow plastic bag and storing all of them in the same box labeled appropriately.

(See color plate #7, Dyed Calf Tails.)

Calf tails on drying bar

7
FURS

I must have every kind of natural fur dubbing that is available. Some is dyed, some is bleached, but most of it is in its natural color. Almost all has been tanned, and most of the pieces were acquired from a furrier I once knew who saved all the trims from his work; when he had a grocery bag or two full of scraps he'd give me a call. You'd be surprised how much rabbit is used in fur coats and jackets. In many instances the guard hairs have been cut back so that they are no longer than the underfur. This looks real nice on a fur coat, but the pieces are useless to a fly tyer who wants the fur pieces for tying dry flies, because there is no way to remove the guard hairs. But I didn't throw these pieces away—I saved them for blending nymph dubbing mixes, where guard hairs are desirable.

I'm to the point where I use nothing but rabbit fur on all my dubbed-body dry flies. The underfur on the sides and belly of a rabbit is extremely fine and among the softest of all furs. Beaver is better, but not quite as available and much more expensive. You can get handfuls of rabbit skins for a little pocket change. Better yet, find some supplier who sells a lot of Zonker strips and ask him to grab a handful of each color of scrap belly and side fur and send it to you. He'll be glad to get a few dollars for what was scraps to him but is super dubbing for you. All you will have to do is cut the pieces into strips, remove the guard hairs and either use it as is or blend the colors you want. I'll talk more about blending in the chapter on mixing and blending furs.

There are some rabbit growers who raise rabbits for restaurants. Many of these animals have snow-white skins. Get your hands on a half dozen or so of these skins and you'll have a supply of dubbing fur that will last a lifetime. Understand that these skins will probably be air dried and may contain a lot of dried animal fat. White rabbit often has fewer guard hairs on the back and very dense underfur. I think it's worth the effort and time it takes to degrease and dye pieces of this fur for dry-fly dubbing.

Degreasing

I use one quarter cup each of Downy liquid, Joy, and Wisk laundry detergent in a three-gallon bucket of hot tap water to degrease air-dried rabbit skins. The concentration can be increased if you have some very oily skins, but the above mixture should work for three or four skins at a time. Remember to scrape as much animal fat off the skins as possible before putting them in the degreasing solution. If the fur around the edges of the skin feels sticky and is discolored from fats and oils, use a razor blade to cut away a thin strip all the way around the skin. The less fat and oil that that goes into the degreasing solution, the better it will work. Leave the skins in this solution for at least two days, stirring periodically. In about a day, you may notice a yellowish film floating on the surface of your degreasing solution. This is an indication that the fats and oils are loosening and coming to the surface. It doesn't mean that the whole batch is getting rotten.

I don't leave the skins in the degreasing solution for more than three days because I'm afraid the hair will begin to loosen and fall out. Remove the skins one at a time and rinse each one very thoroughly under warm tap water. Try to remove as much of the soapy solution as possible. Roll the skin in paper towels to blot away as much excess moisture as possible, then use your hair dryer to dry the hair side of the skin. Do not wring or twist or you'll tear what is now a very soft skin.

Once you have dried the hair side of the skin, you'll be able to determine which part of the skin you want to dye. I wouldn't recommend trying to dye the entire skin in one dye bath. You'll end up with so much dubbing fur of one color that you'll never use it all. I usually cut a full rabbit skin into four pieces, then cut one of the quarter sections into three-quarter-inch-wide strips for dyeing. One fourth of a rabbit skin provides an ample amount of dubbing and by cutting the quarter piece into strips, I have pieces that are easy to work with when they are dry. They also dye more thoroughly since there are more edges for the dye to work into. Since the skins will be very soft after degreasing, I think it is best to remove the guard hairs after the strips have been dyed and are partially dry.

Carefully brush the fur to its natural lie on the remaining three quarter pieces and press them between layers of newspapers as discussed in drying necks. The dried skin will become quite stiff and will be a lot easier to store and cut into strips later if the skins are perfectly flat.

If you have tanned white rabbit hides, you can forget all about the degreasing method discussed above because the tanning process removes all the fats and oils from both the skin and the fur. All you need to do with a tanned rabbit skin is cut it into quarters, cut one quarter piece into three-quarter-inch strips, remove the guard hairs from each strip, soak the strips for a couple of hours in warm

Quartered rabbit skin

water and Downy fabric softener, rinse, and dye. It's rather easy to remove the guard hairs from the narrow strips. Simply grip the tips of the guard hairs between your thumb and forefinger and give them a quick tug. It doesn't take long to remove all the guard hairs from several strips of rabbit fur. You should remove the guard hairs from the strips before you soak them in the Downy and water solution. (See photos on next page)

Dyeing

Select a dyeing recipe from Chapter 9. Carefully mix the dye or dyes and white vinegar and adjust the heat control to 140 degrees F. Cut a small piece from one of the strips you are going to dye and test dye it. The test piece will also give you an idea of how the dye

Pulling guard hairs from strip

Rabbit strips with and without guard hairs

reacts to your material. When you think the test piece is dark enough, remove it from the dye bath, rinse under cold water, then under hot, squeeze in a folded paper towel and dry the fur with your hair dryer. If you got it right, put all the fur pieces in the bath at the same time. If the dye bath needs some adjustments for color or tint, keep test dyeing small pieces until you're satisfied that the dye bath is exactly as you want it.

It is best to dye nothing but white furs, as you'll get cleaner and brighter colors. However, you can dye light gray or light tan furs to shades of color that are darker than the fur's natural color. It is important that you take a little time to study the color wheel before you try this. You can achieve some beautiful deep olives and dirty oranges by dyeing naturally colored furs.

I try to resist the temptation to dye any fur that already has a natural color like ginger, steel gray, slate gray, tan, or brown because it is so easy to alter these colors by mixing them in a blender with fur that is already dyed. These same natural colors are often what is needed to tint some dyed furs before the dyed color is just right. For example, if you have a skin with a natural color of light creamy tan, you can make some beautiful Light Hendrickson dubbing by adding just a pinch of pink dyed rabbit to five or six pinches of the creamy tan.

Drying

Remove all the pieces from the dye bath when they have reached the color you desire. Rinse them under cold tap water to set the dye, then under hot tap water to remove any excess dye particles clinging to the fur and the skin. If you dyed air-dried hides, you probably should rinse the fur pieces in a weak soapy solution of one teaspoon of Joy liquid and one gallon of warm water. The degreasing never really gets all the oils from the air-dried hides and more of these oils will have cooked out during dyeing. There will be some oils on the fur and this will remove most of them. Swirl the dyed pieces around in the soapy rinse a few times and then rinse under lukewarm tap water, gently squeezing and releasing as the water runs over the fur. Tanned fur pieces need not be rinsed in a weak soapy solution because there are no oils left in those skins.

Squeeze as much excess water from the dyed pieces as possible, then roll them in folded paper towels and blot by squeezing firmly. Do not twist or wring the pieces because these skins will also be soft enough to tear. Use your hair dryer to dry the fur side only. If you dyed air-dried fur, examine each piece carefully to determine if there is any oil clinging to the outside edges of the fur. You can easily tell if this has happened because the hairs along the outside edges of the dyed pieces will appear damp, yet the hair dryer won't seem to dry them. Take a single-edge razor blade and cut this very thin strip of skin and fur away from the rest of the dyed piece. If you dyed tanned fur pieces, there will be no problem with oils on the fur.

After you have dried the fur side, place the pieces on several layers of folded newspapers and carefully stroke the hair on the skin to its natural lie. Place several more layers of newspapers on top

Oils on dyed rabbit hair

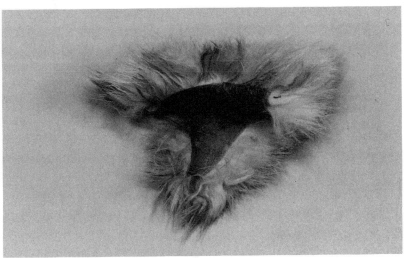

and store for two or three days. Change the papers that come in direct contact with the pieces every half day or so. Keep in mind that the skin portion of these dyed pieces will become very brittle when completely dry. There will also be some significant shrinkage of the skin. The time to remove guard hairs from these dyed pieces is before they are bone dry. I usually pull the guard hairs when the pieces have dried to a point where they are not quite as stiff as a thin piece of cardboard.

8

BLEACHING

I have long admired the beautiful creams and honey blond colors of some of the bleached fly-tying materials I sometimes find in fly shops. There are bleached cock pheasant tail feathers, bleached beaver, bleached elk and deer body hair, and a host of other materials. I seldom use these materials in their bleached state, but it occurred to me that once the natural dark brown and gray colors are removed, it should be a simple matter to dye these hairs, furs, and feathers to some colors that would be of special value because of the materials' texture. I read everything I could get my hands on that might give some hints on how to do this. I even talked to some suppliers, who were very hesitant to offer any information I could use. Even piecing together the occasional hints I got didn't give me enough to start experimenting.

Then one lucky day several years ago, I met an angler and fly tyer who just happened to be the manager of a beauty supply store. Not only did the store offer hair treatments to its customers, it also sold the supplies to those who wanted to bleach and color their hair at home. After buying him several cups of coffee and a bagel or two, I was able to extract just enough information (and supplies) to try my own bleaching. My theory was that if the chemicals were safe enough to use on a person's head, they should be safe enough to use on fly-tying materials without ruining the delicate furs and fibers, and my new friend agreed.

I purchased a bottle of forty percent volume peroxide and a one-pound container of Clairol Basic Professional White, Extra Strength Powder Lightener. (The five percent peroxide that is available at your drugstore or grocery is not powerful enough for our use.) On the way home, I stopped at the grocery and bought a quart of household ammonia. I got out all the notes I had accumulated over the years about bleaching and concocted the following formula:

Mix six scoops (a small plastic scoop comes in the Clairol can) of Clairol lightener with a little hot water to make a paste. Keep thinning this paste until you have a two-cup container of a thin milky solution. The powder has a very strong odor and I don't think it's very wise to inhale it. Be careful not to create a dust cloud when handling the powder. (There are some cautions to this effect printed on the container. Read and observe them carefully.) Pour this solution into your dyeing pan. Then:

- Add one cup of forty percent volume peroxide and mix the two ingredients thoroughly.
- Add one half cup ammonia and mix thoroughly.
- Add four cups hot tap water and mix thoroughly again.

Turn on the exhaust fan if you have one, or open a couple of windows, to allow the ammonia and Clairol fumes to escape. I suppose one could get a little "dingy" if you used this stuff on a daily basis, but I don't think there is any harm in playing around with it once or twice a year. Use your head and try to keep from breathing the fumes.

The above mixture is enough to complete a number of bleaching chores. I use it primarily to bleach cream hackles to white and I always do that first, while the mixture is at its peak strength. Then I will throw in a couple of strips of deer or elk body hair, or a couple of grizzly rooster or hen necks. It will also bleach moose body hair, fox squirrel tails, black bear body hair, even peccary. The latest use I have for it is bleaching brown dry-fly necks to ginger! A few years ago, brown dry-fly necks were very scarce and we had to learn to dye ginger necks to brown. Now the situation has reversed and ginger necks seem to be few while brown necks are plentiful. However, be warned that bleaching brown to ginger is rather tricky and time consuming. If you bleach the brown neck too long in an attempt to achieve a light honey ginger, you'll probably ruin the neck. All the hackle fibers will begin to curl and appear much thinner. Try this on a piece of old neck butt that contains roughly the same quality of feathers as the neck you wish to bleach to determine if you really want to chance it on an expensive #1 or #2 dry-fly neck.

Regardless of what material you wish to bleach, first be sure that every feather or hair has been thoroughly soaked in a warm, weak soapy solution. This is not an attempt to remove any oils from the fur or feathers but is intended to make certain that everything is wet and will bleach more quickly and completely. Soak the materials for only a few minutes, then rinse the soapy solution from them under warm tap water and put them into the dye pan holding your bleaching solution.

Make sure that all the feathers or hair are saturated with the bleaching solution. Turn the material often and press the solution into the material with your fingers. (You should, of course, be wearing your rubber gloves.) Periodically lift the material from the bleach and squeeze all the solution from it, and then put the material back. This will help to ensure that there are fresh bleaching chemicals in direct contact with the material for longer periods of time.

Try to keep the bleaching solution at about 100 degrees Fahrenheit — no hotter. *Never* reheat the solution on your hot plate while the materials you're bleaching are still in the pan. Remove the material, reheat the solution, remove the pan from the hot plate, and then put the material back in the pan. Since the liquid volume of the bleaching solution is not very great, there is a strong possibility that the coils of your hot plate will create hot spots on the pan that will ruin any hackle fiber or hair that touches them.

You will be the judge of when the materials are *bleached* light enough. I have never been able bleach natural gray deer hair to snow white, for example. I'm not even sure it's possible. But you *can* achieve some very light honey gingers from almost all natural hairs and feathers. The trick is to remove as much natural color as possible without ruining the fibers. *Never* attempt to bleach with Clorox, as it destroys fibers.

Rinse the bleached material very thoroughly, first under warm tap water for several minutes, alternately squeezing and releasing the material to flush as much of the bleaching solution out as possible. Then mix a weak soapy solution of one teaspoon liquid Joy dishwashing detergent and one gallon of warm water and swirl the bleached material in it for several more minutes. Rinse completely and squeeze to remove the excess water. Blot the material in folded paper towels and use your hair dryer to dry all but the skin side. Either press the material between layers of newspapers or hang from a drying bar as outlined earlier.

Manufacturers of some of the products sold in beauty supply stores will no longer sell to anyone but a professional hairdresser, since some people have misused the products (on their heads), burned their scalps, and sued the maker for damages. To protect themselves from further abuse, the companies have withdrawn some of their products from sales to the consumer. You'll have be very careful how you acquire some of the materials I have listed above. It could cost you several dozen flies at the very least, or possibly the exact location of one of your favorite fishing spots. If you can get your hands on this material, don't tell even your closest buddy where you got it. There are a lot of very understanding folks involved in our sport, and with a little discreet questioning you'll be able to find a supplier.

(See color plate #8, Bleached Materials.)

9

DYE
MIXES
and
RECIPES

Rit powder dyes contain a great deal of salt, which must be dissolved before you can use the dye. Rit liquid dyes also contain salt, but it is already dissolved and suspended with the dissolved particles of dye. The significance of the choice between liquid or powder is that there is a major difference in the amount of dye of either type you will use for a specific dyeing job. The label on the back of a 1 1/8-ounce box of Rit powder dye indicates that one package of dry powder will dye one pound of dry weight, or about three yards of medium-weight fabric. The eight-ounce bottle of concentrated Rit liquid dye will dye two pounds of dry weight. To further compound this difference, you seldom need to use an entire package of dry dye. Since salt particles are heavier than dye particles, it is entirely possible that one day you may measure out a teaspoon of dry dye and get ninety-eight percent salt and two percent dye particles. Some days or weeks later you may measure another teaspoon of dye from the same package and get eighty percent salt and twenty percent dye particles. Considering the enormous difference in dye strength between two percent and twenty percent, I'm sure you can guess what the result might be if you attempt to match colors from previous dyeing chores.

You can solve this problem by making your own liquid working solution from the powder dyes. Empty two packages of dry Rit dye (same color!) into a coffee carafe, add one cup of water and bring to a slow simmering boil. Stir and simmer until all the salt and dye particles have dissolved. You may notice a scum line develop around the inside of the carafe; it contains impurities from the dissolved salt and dye, and perhaps some weird stuff from your water. Don't be too concerned about this. Keep stirring until you're convinced that not all the particles are going to dissolve and remove the carafe from the hot plate to cool a little before pouring the liquid into a plastic bottle for storage. Boiling hot liquid could melt the thin walls of some plastic bottles and cause a terrible spill. When that happens, you are faced with a major clean-up and the fiercest wrath from all others who inhabit your house. Using a funnel will also reduce the chances of spilling. When I pour the liquid dye from my carafe into a plastic bottle, I always set the bottle *in* the sink, just in case. That little precaution has saved me from major embarassment on several occasions. You can either save plastic juice bottles or buy them at your local hardware store. The only caution I would offer here is to make certain that the plastic bottles you choose have screw-on caps. Snap-on caps also snap off, usually at the worst time.

You have now made your own liquid dye working solution. Every time you measure a teaspoon or tablespoon of this solution into your dye bath, you can be absolutely certain of the strength because all the ingredients have been dissolved. To be on the safe side, I give the bottle a couple of shakes before measuring out dye for a bath.

Since we made our solution by disolving two packages of dry dye

Plastic bottles and funnel

(each of which would dye one pound of dry fabric) in one cup of water, one would probably be willing to assume that the strength of our solution and liquid Rit is equal, since the label on the eight-ounce liquid dye says it will dye two pounds of dry material. Don't assume, test dye! I think the factory version of the liquid dye is stronger and normally use less of it than I would of the liquid concentrate I make from two packs of disolved dye. A couple of warnings:

- All Rit powder dyes, and only Rit powder dyes, should be disolved into a working solution as described above. You will be measuring small amounts from the working solution to create dye baths using the recipes listed later.
- Never attempt to make a liquid working solution from high-concentrate powder dyes such as Veniard.

Check out the various fly-fishing magazines and other periodicals for advertisements by manufacturers and distributors of high-concentrate powder dyes such as Veniard. This stuff is very powerful and you should be extremely careful when using it. Just a dozen grains spilled on your counter top (or, worse yet, your carpet), will change the color of whatever it's on the instant moisture comes in contact with it. I have found that Formula 409 is great stuff for removing stains left from splatters and spills. Keep these powerful dyes in tightly closed glass or plastic containers and stored away from moisture. If you use glass containers, be certain that you store them someplace where there is no possibility of breakage.

Try to get all your fluorescent dyes from the same supplier. If you can't, find the local supplier of Tintex brand dyes. This company produces dyes that are called "neon green," "neon pink," and "neon yellow," for example. I haven't used them, but I assume (and I know it's dangerous to assume anything), the colors will be what we know as fluorescent. The label on the box says "Manufactured for KIWI BRANDS, INC." But it doesn't say who did the manufacturing. A few days before turning this manuscript in to the publisher, I learned that Rit now manufactures the same three neon colors. Keep your eyes and ears open to new ideas and new products.

Remember the following before you attempt to dye:

- The following dye mixes, recipes, and formulas are (with a few noted exceptions) all added to twenty-five cups of water and one quarter cup of white vinegar.
- Again, with a few noted exceptions, all are meant to dye up to six rooster necks or three bucktails at a time.
- If you wish to dye fewer than six rooster necks or three bucktails, do not decrease any formula by more than fifty percent or use fewer than sixteen cups of water for the dye bath.
- The Rit dye formulas are all based on a standard of making your own working solution from two packages of dry Rit dye and one cup of water as described earlier.
- The temperature of the dye bath should never exceed 140 degrees F.
- All material to be dyed (except tanned hides) should be degreased.
- Rinse all soaked and degreased material thoroughly.

- Constantly stir and turn the material in the dye bath.
- All wet material will appear darker than when dry.
- Be certain that all excess dye has been washed away before drying and storing the dyed material.
- You must have white to dye to bright!
- The quality of your water supply may affect some of the recipes.
- Clean your bamboo tongs with Formula 409 and a sponge under hot water before you handle any light colored material in the dye bath. There will always be a residue of dye on the arms and tips of your tongs from the last dyeing session. If you don't clean your tongs, you may put dark marks on your white bucktails or cream/white rooster necks.
- Always clean the dye pan with Formula 409 and paper towels after each dye bath. Rinse with hot tap water and dry.
- Never save used dye.

You should have some understanding of the color wheel that artists use when they mix their paints. Check out a book on color from your library and read it just to get a little understanding of colors and how they react to each other. Grumbacher produces a color wheel (Cat. No. B 420) that shows you what you get when you add colors together. It's a color-computing device that has a rotating disc with windows in it. Choose a color to add to another and the window will show you what color the mix will produce. It's an invaluable tool when you want to mix dyes to produce different shades. Write to M. Grumbacher, Inc., 460 West 34th Street, New York, NY 10001 to find the name and address of the nearest distributor of their products.

Mixes and Recipes

Light dun from cream white rooster necks or saddles
2 tablespoons Rit pearl grey #39
3/4 tablespoon Rit tan #16

Medium dun from cream white rooster necks or saddles

5 tablespoons Rit pearl grey #39

1 ½ tablespoons Rit tan #16

Slate dun from cream white rooster necks or saddles

8 tablespoons Rit pearl grey #39

2 ½ tablespoons Rit tan #16

Medium dun from domestic cream white hen or pullet necks or backs

4 tablespoons Rit pearl grey #39

1 tablespoon Rit tan #16

Regular brown from medium ginger rooster necks or saddles

2 tablespoons Rit cocoa brown #20

(less than) ¼ teaspoon Veniard Summer Duck

Note: This is a recipe I found in one of Eric Leiser's books.

Coachman brown from medium ginger rooster necks or saddles

3 tablespoons Rit cocoa brown #20

¼ tablespoon Veniard Summer Duck

It takes a little more time to dye to Coachman brown and you may have to add a fourth tablespoon of Rit cocoa brown to the dye bath to achieve the deep, dark, reddish brown quality of a true Coachman brown.

Wood-duck flank from mallard flank

10 cups water

1 cup wet flank feathers

1 tablespoon Rit tan #16

2 tablespoons white vinegar

Olive green
  2 tablespoons Rit Kelly green #32
  ¹/₂ tablespoon Rit tan #16
  ¹/₂ tablespoon Rit gold #23

This recipe originally called for 1 ¹/₂ tablespoons of Rit avacado green and one teaspoon of Rit Kelly green. Rit avacado is no longer available, so you will have to adjust the amount of Kelly green and tan to achieve the right tint of olive. Remember that there is a lot of red dye in tan; If you add too much, you will begin to turn your dye bath gray as the green and red particles begin to neutralize each other.

Salmon fly orange (dirty orange)
  ¹/₄ teaspoon Veniard orange
  ¹/₈ teaspoon Veniard Summer Duck

Grass shrimp blue (bonefish)
  1 tablespoon Rit royal blue #29

Whistler pink (saltwater)
  7 tablespoons Rit rose pink #7
  1 teaspoon Rit scarlet #5

Light tan calf tail from natural white
  2 tablespoons Rit tan #16

Light tan turkey T-base from natural white
  2 tablespoons Rit tan #16
  (20 cups water, 2 cups wet turkey)

Fluorescent chartreuse from any pure white natural material
  ³/₄ teaspoon Veniard fluorescent yellow
  ¹/₄ teaspoon Veniard fluorescent lime green

Sulphur dun wings from domestic cream white hen or pullet necks

> *First* dye with 3 tablespoons Rit yellow #1
> *then* over-dye with 3 tablespoons Rit gray #39

Experiment with one ratty old neck to find the right "wet" color of yellow on the first dye. (You want a neck with a slight yellowish cast to it.) Then, immerse the same neck in the gray dye bath to put the slight tinges of gray to each feather that the natural insect has on its wings. It only takes a few moments in the gray dye bath to achieve this effect. These are beautiful necks when you get them right. I would strongly suggest that you dye only one neck at a time, as it's very easy to get both colors too dark.

Pale morning dun wings from cream white hen or pullet necks

> *First* dye with 1 tablespoon Rit tan #16
> *then* over-dye with 1 tablespoon Rit pearl gray #39

Use the same over-dyeing technique described above for sulphur dun wings. The first dye should result in a very light cream to light tan cast. The second dye should add tinges of gray to each feather, but not cover the light tan.

Bright green (not fluorescent) from any pure white natural material

> 3 tablespoons Rit dark green #35
> ³/₄ teaspoon Veniard fluorescent lime green

Light blue (soft hackle for steelhead flies)

> 10 cups water
> 1 tablespoon Rit light blue #26
> 8 cream white hen neck butts

Purple from any natural cream white material

> 4 tablespoons Rit navy blue #30
> 1 tablespoon Rit scarlet #5

Yellow bucktails
> 3 bucktails
> 1 teaspoon Veniard yellow

Red bucktails
> 3 bucktails
> 1 teaspoon Veniard bright red

Blue bucktails
> 1 tablespoon Rit royal blue #29 for each bucktail
> An additional tablespoon of Rit navy blue #30 will deepen the color

Black from any natural material
> *First* dye to very dark brown or red.
> *Then* over-dye to black using one tablespoon of Rit black for each neck, or two tablespoons of Rit black for each bucktail. It takes a long time to get a good deep black. You'll probably have to add more dye to the dye bath and leave the materials in it for most of the day. (This is the only time you don't have to worry about adding fresh dye to a partially used dye bath.) Agitate and turn the material every ten minutes to ensure that the dye is getting down to the base of each hair or feather. Keep in mind that the water in your dye bath will evaporate and you'll have to keep adding water, or the heat from your hot plate could ruin the material you're dyeing.

Medium brown grizzly for bass bugs
> 1 tablespoon Rit tan #16
> 1 teaspoon Rit cocoa brown #20
> 1 teaspoon Rit gold #23

Green drake grizzly
> 2 tablespoons Rit Kelly green #32
> 1 tablespoon Rit tan #16
> 1/8 teaspoon Veniard yellow

The above recipes will help with most of your dyeing. By the time you have tried all of them, you'll no doubt have discovered some other colors you'd like to try. Don't be afraid to experiment. And be sure to keep accurate notes on how much of each dye, which kind of dye, and how much water you used.

You'll find several degrees of hardness to the quality of some materials. Harder materials seem to resist accepting a dye. Have patience — all natural materials can be dyed.

Dyeing Stripped Hackle Quills

The following recipes are based on ten cups of water and two tablespoons of white vinegar mixed in a coffee carafe. Each recipe will dye up to six bundles of stripped rooster hackle quills.

Medium blue dun from white
1 tablespoon Rit gray #39

Medium brown from white
1 tablespoon Rit tan #16

Pale yellow from white
1/8 teaspoon Veniard yellow

Cream from white
1 teaspoon Rit tan #16

Olive quill from white
(for *Baetis* & Blue-winged olive bodies)
First dye with 1/8 teaspoon Veniard yellow
Then over-dye with 1 tablespoon Rit Kelly green #32

The first dye should produce a yellowish cast to the quills. The second dye should produce light green quills with some of the yellow showing through. Early and late-season naturals will be darker in color; summer naturals will be lighter. Dye your quills accordingly. To dye the quill bundles darker, simply leave them in each dye bath a little longer.

Melon Quill pink from white
1 tablespoon Rit rose pink #7

Dyeing Notes

Use the following charts to record your quantities and procedures. They will come in handy in the future if you repeat a recipe.

COLOR _____ FROM _____
MATERIAL AMOUNT _____
WATER _____ CUPS
DYE FORMULA _____
_____
_____
_____

COLOR _____ FROM _____
MATERIAL AMOUNT _____
WATER _____ CUPS
DYE FORMULA _____
_____
_____
_____

(See color plate #9, Stripped and Dyed Hackle Quills.)

Dyeing Notes

COLOR _____ FROM _____

MATERIAL AMOUNT _____

WATER _____ CUPS

DYE FORMULA _____

_____

_____

_____

COLOR _____ FROM _____

MATERIAL AMOUNT _____

WATER _____ CUPS

DYE FORMULA _____

_____

_____

_____

COLOR _____ FROM _____

MATERIAL AMOUNT _____

WATER _____ CUPS

DYE FORMULA _____

_____

_____

_____

Dyeing Notes

COLOR _____ FROM _____
MATERIAL AMOUNT _____
WATER _____ CUPS
DYE FORMULA _____
_____
_____
_____

COLOR _____ FROM _____
MATERIAL AMOUNT _____
WATER _____ CUPS
DYE FORMULA _____
_____
_____
_____

COLOR _____ FROM _____
MATERIAL AMOUNT _____
WATER _____ CUPS
DYE FORMULA _____
_____
_____
_____

Dyeing Notes

COLOR _____ FROM _____

MATERIAL AMOUNT _____

WATER _____ CUPS

DYE FORMULA _____

_____

_____

_____

COLOR _____ FROM _____

MATERIAL AMOUNT _____

WATER _____ CUPS

DYE FORMULA _____

_____

_____

_____

COLOR _____ FROM _____

MATERIAL AMOUNT _____

WATER _____ CUPS

DYE FORMULA _____

_____

_____

_____

Dyeing Notes

COLOR _____ FROM _____

MATERIAL AMOUNT _____

WATER _____ CUPS

DYE FORMULA _____

_____

_____

_____

COLOR _____ FROM _____

MATERIAL AMOUNT _____

WATER _____ CUPS

DYE FORMULA _____

_____

_____

_____

COLOR _____ FROM _____

MATERIAL AMOUNT _____

WATER _____ CUPS

DYE FORMULA _____

_____

_____

_____

Dyeing Notes

COLOR _____ FROM _____

MATERIAL AMOUNT _____

WATER _____ CUPS

DYE FORMULA _____

_____

_____

_____

COLOR _____ FROM _____

MATERIAL AMOUNT _____

WATER _____ CUPS

DYE FORMULA _____

_____

_____

_____

COLOR _____ FROM _____

MATERIAL AMOUNT _____

WATER _____ CUPS

DYE FORMULA _____

_____

_____

_____

10

COLOR REMOVAL

D on't throw away any of your dyeing mistakes, especially if you used Rit dye. The Rit Dye Company and Tintex both market a product called "Color Remover," and it works pretty well. Neither product will remove all the color from the material you have dyed, but they'll get most of it — enough that you can over-dye the material to a different shade or tint from your original dye job. If you don't want to remove the color from a previous dye job you should save your dyeing mistakes anyway, because you can dye anything to black.

A few years ago I needed some large, bright green grizzly-neck butt feathers for some saltwater flies I wanted to tie, but didn't have the right feathers to dye since I was between shipments of grizzly necks. I did have a box of green grizzly neck butts left over from tying a lot of Green Drakes, but the color wasn't bright or light enough. I'm sure you can see the problem I was faced with.

I tried Rit Color Remover on the Green Drake grizzly-neck butts, thinking that if it worked I could re-dye the necks to a ligher and brighter color. It worked so well that I now recycle a lot of dyed necks that no longer have feathers of the right size. After only thirty or forty minutes, the eight dark green grizzly-neck butts I had put in the color remover solution were nearly back to their original natural color. There were still traces of a sickly looking yellowish green, but after another fifteen or twenty minutes I couldn't detect any appreciable additional fading of color, so I thoroughly rinsed the neck butts and re-dyed them with a mixture of fluorescent lime green and Rit Kelly green. The result was a perfect match to my pattern sample. I have since learned to pull and size the hackles I will need for a specific pattern and dye them as loose feathers. It saves a lot of time and material.

Both Rit and Tintex color removers are quite strong chemicals. If you use too much of them you can curl the individual hackle fibers on every hackle stem. You could easily ruin every neck you put into this solution unless you mix it properly. Also, the dry powders produce a strong odor when mixed with hot water to make the solution. Use this stuff near an open window or have an exhaust fan nearby to remove most of the fumes. There are no cautions on the package about breathing the fumes, so perhaps they're only a little obnoxious to keep you at a safe distance. There are some cautions about getting the material in your eyes and about "prolonged" skin contact. Wear glasses and rubber gloves. You should be wearing rubber gloves *any time* you are dyeing materials.

The Tintex package contains 1.9 ounces of dry color remover. According to the instruction sheet inside the box, this is enough color remover to treat one pound of material that is completely covered with water. Since a few neck butts weigh only a couple of ounces, I tried a formula of one tablespoon of dry color remover to eight cups of hot tap water, and it worked fine.

Pour eight cups of hot water into your dye pan, add one table-spoon of dry color remover and stir until all the powder has dissolved. This will be enough solution to remove most of the dyed color from five necks. Since you are attempting to remove color from some previously dyed material, there is no need to use the complete degreasing process as outlined earlier. Simply soak the material in lukewarm water for ten or fifteen minutes to make sure every hair or feather is wet.

Put the necks (or other material) into the solution all at once. Stir and turn the pieces frequently to make sure that fresh color remover is in contact with the material at all times. Try to keep the temperature of this solution no higher than 120 degrees. If you need to reheat the solution on your hot plate, remove the neck butts first, as there is not enough volume to the solution to keep the neck butts away from the very hot bottom of the pan as you re-heat it.

You may find that using only one tablespoon of color remover to eight cups of water will be a rather weak solution, and that it may take a while longer than thirty or forty minutes to remove as much color as you'd like. You may add small amounts of additional color remover to the solution, but I wouldn't add more than half a tea-spoon at a time, and I'd give the original solution at least an hour's time to work before you add more. Remember, it is entirely poss-ible to ruin the feather fibers if the solution is too strong. Remove all the necks from the solution before you add more color remover powder and stir thoroughly to be sure all the powder has dissolved.

Rinse any material that you have put in a color removal solution very thoroughly before you attempt to re-dye it. Wash it in a gallon of warm water with a teaspoon of Joy liquid and then rinse under warm tap water until you're certain all the color remover has been washed away. Any color remover remaining on your materials will weaken the dye; the dye bath will certainly not perform as well as it would with untreated material.

The instruction sheet that comes in the package of Tintex Color Remover contains a handy little chart of what colors should result when you use some common dye colors to dye material that has already been dyed to another common color. Pin this chart to the wall in your dyeing room; it's a good guide and will help you to understand how colors react to each other.

11

STRIPPING QUILLS

I think that stripped peacock or stripped rooster hackle quills make far more realistic mayfly bodies than any other material. The finished fly has prominent segmentation, a finely tapered, carrot-shaped abdomen, and a smooth waxy surface, and it floats like a tiny cork. We can make the same observations about nearly all natural mayflies. Contrary to what seems to be a rather popular opinion, stripped quills are not so fragile as to make them an impractical tying material. If you really believe that, then I offer the opinion that perhaps one of two things happened to the quills you used: (1) they were very old and brittle before stripping; and (2) the quills were damaged during stripping. When you need to tie a half dozen Blue Quills for tomorrow's outing, and it's already 11:00 P.M., either of those possibilities will significantly affect both the quality and length of the sleep you'll get tonight.

Taking a little extra time and care in selecting all of your fly-tying materials will always pay off with materials that are easier to work with and better looking, more durable flies. I like to hand pick all the peacock I think I'm going to strip for bodies. Choose those feathers that contain the thickest herls. This doesn't always mean they will be longer; often the longer herls will also be the thinnest and most fragile. I have found that there is about five or six inches of good, heavy herls on either side of the feather just below the eye. (You will occasionally find some feathers that have sturdy herls well up into the eye on both sides of the center quill.)

You may have to look at as many as twenty or thirty feathers to find six or eight that you can use for stripping. Not all peacocks are alike, nor were their diets or their environment, just as each tail feather is not identical — even though they appear to be so when we see photos of a male peacock in full courting display. Next time you see such a photo, look at the individual feathers, not the full display, and you will begin to have a bettter understanding of the variety of quality there can be.

There are three or four methods of removing the fuzzy green stuff from the individual peacock herls. One is to pinch one herl at a time between your thumb and forefinger and strip the fuzz with your thumbnail. It takes a long time to make even a small pile of stripped quills this way. I usually break most of them because I either pinch too hard or I get careless when I try to hurry the job.

A second method of stripping the individual herl is to use a pencil eraser. All you need is a clean counter or desktop and a soft pencil eraser of the type and size that you hold in your hand (not the one stuck on the end of a wood pencil). Hold the tip end of the herl down with the index finger of one hand and stroke the herl with the eraser. The pulling action of the rubber eraser rubs the green fuzz off the stem much faster than your thumbnail. I find I break a lot of herls because I either apply too much pressure, or try to hurry, or both. I also find that many of the herls twist, and there is often a

Stripping herl with thumbnail

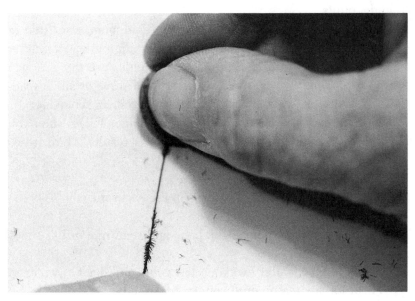

Stripping herl with eraser

half inch of fuzz on one side in about the middle of the quill that won't let go.

A third method is buying waxed peacock eyes. I tried this once, and I'll never try it again. The first and most important thing wrong with this idea is that it is impossible for you to determine the quality of the herl. The second is that there is always too much wax on the herls and they are stuck together. Just try to separate them without breaking them. If you use hot water to soften the wax, you've added another step to the whole process, because you must still remove the wax by pulling the herl between your thumb and forefinger. The theory is that the green fuzz will come off with the wax, and it does, but I found that I was breaking even more quills than when I used my thumbnail or an eraser. Perhaps there is some secret about doing this, but I haven't learned yet.

I'm convinced that the best way to remove the fuzz from peacock herl is to use a solution of Clorox and hot tap water. The Clorox solution will disolve or "burn" the green fuzz from all the herls in just a few seconds. If done correctly, you will not weaken the individual herl quills and you will not remove a significant amount of color from the quills.

To burn peacock quills you need some equipment not listed in Chapter 1. An old cake pan and one wide-mouth one-quart fruit jar should be pretty easy to find in most basements. Use the cake pan for the Clorox and water solution; the jar will serve as an "inspection" jar. Use a one-gallon plastic pail as a neutralizing container.

There are some absolute rules that you cannot fudge when you burn peacock quills or you'll have disastrous results. They are as follows:

- Lock the cat in the garage.
- Tie the dog to the sturdiest tree in the backyard.
- Send the kids next door.
- Give your spouse the check book and send him or her shopping.
- Lock all doors after everyone has gone, and don't answer the door for any reason until you have finished.
- Take the phone off the hook.

Cake pan & wide-mouth jar

Got that? You are ready to begin.

Select your six to eight peacock eyes with the heaviest herls and clip away the remaining butt section of each feather. Save these for use as streamer topping or body herl on Royal Coachmen.

Mix a solution of one fourth Clorox and three fourths hot water. A four cup solution in a standard size cake pan will produce a liquid depth of about $^5/_8$ inch, which will be more than adequate to burn a dozen peacock eyes.

Fill the one-quart wide-mouth jar with clear tap water. This will be your inspection jar.

Fill a one-gallon pail with warm tap water and add two tablespoons of baking soda. Stir until all the powder has dissolved. This solution will neutralize any remaining traces of Clorox after burning and rinsing.

Take one peacock eye and swish it in the Clorox solution. Remove the eye from the solution the moment you notice that it has begun to fizz. Rinse the eye thoroughly under warm tap water and then place the rinsed eye into the inspection jar. If there are still small patches or tufts of green fuzz remaining on some of the herl quills, replace the eye in the Clorox solution, give it two or three swirls and remove and repeat rinsing and inspection until all the herls have been burned clean. But be very careful when you put the peacock eye back into the Clorox that it is in the solution for only two or three seconds. Once all the green fuzz has been removed, the only thing remaining for the Clorox to destroy is the quill itself. The enamel coating on the quill portion of a peacock herl is very thin; once the Clorox has had an opportunity to damage it, the quills will be useless to you because they'll crack in a thousand places as you wind them around the shank of a hook.

When you are satisfied that all the herls have been cleaned of all the green fuzz, rinse the eye very thoroughly under warm tap water and place it in the baking soda solution to neutralize any remaining traces of Clorox.

Now that you have burned one peacock eye, you will have a pretty good idea how the process works and what to look for. Put all the remaining eyes into the Clorox solution at the same time and repeat the procedure for burning just one eye. It won't take but a few seconds longer to burn all the eyes than it did to burn just one. When all the eyes are completely stripped, rinse them thoroughly under warm tap water and place them in the baking soda solution. Allow them to neutralize for five or ten minutes while you clean up. Rinse them again under warm tap water and the stripped quills are ready for use. You can dye these stripped quills to a beautiful olive green if you wish. Or, if you think the burning process has removed some of the natural dark brownish dun color, you can easily replace the lost color by dyeing the quills in a dye bath of tan and gray. Mix one tablespoon Rit tan #16 and two tablespoons Rit pearl gray #39 in eight cups of water and a dash of white vinegar. The original color should be restored in only two or three minutes.

Stripping rooster neck butt hackles for making quill bodies is a different matter entirely. The individual feathers contain fibers that are much sturdier, so you'll be using a more concentrated solution

Burning peacock

of Clorox and water to remove them. The butt hackle feathers will be bundled with a rubber band first at the tips and then at the butts, and this requires a different method of handling in the burning process. And, since the total length of the material to be stripped is far less than peacock eyes, you'll be using smaller volumes of all the solutions needed to burn and neutralize the quills.

Careful selection of the butt feathers to be stripped is quite important. I try to find neck butts that have the longest and thickest diameter butt hackles, with lots of web along each side of the quill. I can tie larger flies with the thicker hackle stems and the soft webby feathers will burn clean a lot faster than hard, shiny hackle fibers. Choose natural dun for use as body material for the Blue Quill, natural medium ginger for Ginger Quill bodies, or natural brown for Red Quills. If any of the neck butts you choose for stripping were dyed necks, the burning process will remove all the dyed color from the quills and you'll be back to the natural color of the neck. I prefer to strip only cream/white neck butts because then I can dye the stripped quills to any color I might need.

Pull only the longest feathers from the butt of the neck and place them in a six- to-eight-inch-long plastic box that has a lid. (Don't bother pulling any feather that is shorter than 3 1/2 inches. They're too short to comfortably work with, and the stems are too thin.) Close the lid of the box and tap it against the heel of your hand to align all the butts. Carefully open the lid and remove all the feathers at the same time. Use a small rubber band to bind the tips of the hackles together as shown in the photo below.

Don't mix the feathers from two or three necks in the same bundle, because there will be a difference in the hardness of the hackle fibers of each neck and they won't burn at the same rate. You could easily ruin all the hackles from one neck butt as you attempt to burn off all the fibers from the hackles of another neck if both are in the same clump. Binding the clump of feathers at the tip allows the butts to flare slightly, which seems to aid in the removal of the fibers near the butts of the feathers since the Clorox can easily flow around all the butts. I usually make two to four bundles of

Hackles bound at tips

feathers before I begin the actual burning to make the project a little more worthwhile. Try to keep the bundles to a size that is no larger in diameter at the butts than a standard lead pencil. More mass than that will result in some incomplete burning of the feathers in the middle of the bundle.

(Try to get some strung Chinese or domestic rooster neck hackle. It's usually from four to six inches long (six to eight inches is better) and is very consistent in diameter. Use about 1 ½ inches of feathers per clump. Pull them off the string they're strung on and bind them with a rubber band as described above.)

You'll need three twelve-ounce plastic drinking glasses to burn, inspect and neutralize butt hackles. Mix a solution of one half Clorox and one half hot tap water in one glass for the burning solution. Fill another glass with warm tap water for inspection, and dissolve one tablespoon of baking soda in warm water in the third glass for neutralizing the trace amounts of Clorox that may remain on the quills after rinsing.

Thoroughly wet the clumps under running water before immersing them in the Clorox solution. A quick way to do this is to give

Three labeled glasses

Burning hackle butts

the clump a short shot of 409 and then hold the clump under running water as you squeeze and release the clump.

Immerse the clump butt first into the Clorox solution, and constantly use a stirring motion to be certain that the Clorox is getting to all the fibers in the butt section of each feather. The solution will begin to foam and fizz in just a few seconds. This is an indication that the Clorox is beginning to destroy the fibers near the butts.

When you notice that some of the soft marabou-like fibers are beginning to disappear, remove the clump from the Clorox solution and hold it under hot water so you can see how far things have progressed. Remove the clump from the Clorox solution when all the fibers have disappeared from the bottom third of each hackle stem. Rinse the clump thoroughly, remove the rubber band from the tips and bind the clump at the cleaned butts with the same rubber band. (See photo on next page.)

Dump the Clorox solution and make a fresh mixture for burning the tips. Immerse the tips and continue as above. Constantly swirl and stir until you notice that there are only a few hackle fibers re-

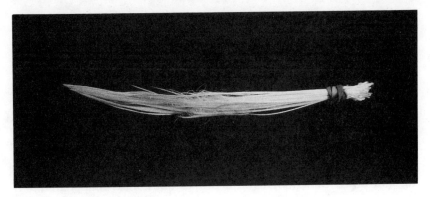

Hackles bound at butts

maining near the tips of each feather. Rinse and immerse the bundle in the inspection glass to see how completely the quills have been cleaned. (Do this often or you could begin to destroy the enamel coating on each hackle quill.) If there are only a few stubborn hackle fibers remaining near the very tips of the quills, you'd be wise to stop burning, as you won't be using the very thin tips of

Burning hackle tips

these quills anyway. More time in the Clorox will begin to destroy the enamel coating on the remainder of the quills. Rinse thoroughly under warm tap water and immerse the stripped clump into the baking soda solution.

Allow the stripped bundle of quills to remain in the baking soda solution for at least fifteen or twenty minutes while you clean up and put things away. You should rinse the neutralized quills under warm tap water before you dye them or tie with them. If the quills feel slick during this rinse, work them with your fingers by stroking up and down their length until the slickness has disappeared. All the chemicals will be gone at this point and the quills are ready to be either dyed or used as they are.

Never remove the rubber band from the butts of the quills until you are ready to tie, and replace the rubber band when you have finished tying. Dried stripped quills are almost impossible to handle for storage as they get very stiff and springy. Leave the rubber band around the butts when you dye the quills as well. Always tie with water-soaked quills and stroke a drop of thin head lacquer along the body after you have finished the fly.

(See color plate #9, Dyed Stripped Hackle Quills.)

Burned hackle quills

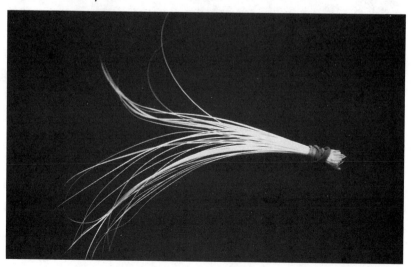

12

FUR

BLENDING

Since this entire book has dealt with dyeing and bleaching tying materials to the appropriate colors for the patterns you want to tie, it seemed logical that I should discuss blending various colored furs to achieve some of the subtle tints we see in so many natural insects. I have never seen an acquatic or terrestrial insect whose body, legs, and wings didn't have a variety of very subtle color changes. The abdomens of many mayflies are prominently ribbed with lighter and darker shades of creamy yellow or creamy light green to dark olive, for example. The same thing can be said of many caddisflies, stoneflies, and midges that trout feed on every day of the year. The color variations can be dramatically different from stream to stream, as well as from season to season.

The number of fly fishers has increased each year for as long as I can remember; anglers' abilities have increased, too. Fish and game management authorities throughout the nation have very wisely designated more miles of special regulation water each year. Some of these areas are no-kill areas, and others have size limit and possession limit combinations that, in effect, make them no-kill areas. I applaud all efforts to preserve the resource. The result of all this is that lot of us have been "educating" a lot of trout over the past two or three decades.

Now, I know that not many trout live as long as a decade, but I have fished to some little ten-inches that were so wary that I would almost be willing to bet that I and others before me had caught their parents many times before. I don't have any scientific data to back up a growing theory in the back of my head that perhaps the spawners are passing some of their wariness (acquired through painful experience) down to their offspring through programmed gene pools. That thought gives a lot of credit to something that has a brain as tiny as a trout's, but then again, it could be a developing instinct. At least that's how I rationalize those days when the trout are feeding and I'm not catching them, while other anglers are. I must be casting to the only new-age trout in the stream. It at least allows me to hike back to the truck with a little of my self-respect intact. I've often thought of clipping the hook off just at the beginning of the bend to see if that little piece of wire could be the tip-off to the trout. I cannot do that because if I did, and it worked, I'd have to tell someone about it, and then word would get around that I had gone over the edge that I'm so close to already.

Given average to above-average casting skills, and the ability to approach the trout without spooking them and present the fly with a long drag-free float, I must build an extra edge into the fly — something that will make it appear as identical as possible to the natural insect, from the trout's perspective. There are a lot of theories about what the trout sees. The research data and resulting theories are all valuable to a point. And one could *ask* the trout. "What does this look like to you?", but no one will hear an answer.

What I do believe is this: If we can dye a quill or mix dubbing that contains as many shades of color as exist on the natural insect from *our* perspective, then chances are it'll appear a lot more like the natural to the trout as well.

The two most valuable pieces of equipment I carry while I'm fishing are my camera and a bug net. The camera is a Pentax K1000, which is all metal and seems to weigh a ton at the end of the day. I use a 50mm macro lens, and can get nearly life-size pictures of insects because of the extreme close-up capability of the lens. When I get back slides from a day of taking pictures of bugs on the stream, and find one good slide out of a roll of twenty-four exposures, I'm damn glad I carried that heavy camera. A ¼-inch mayfly becomes nearly two feet long on an an eight-foot projection screen. I'm always amazed at the gentle shadings of color on the bugs in every slide I put on the screen.

We simply need to learn to look at things the way they really are. Learn to notice the details that make up the whole. How does one component affect another? There is a little exercise you can try on yourself when you're alone that will help you to begin to really see details. (I say when you're alone because if your significant other catches you doing this, you too may be accused of having gone over the edge.) Lay one hand on your desk top and begin to count all the wrinkles and lines on the back of your hand, starting with the thumb. Then go back and begin counting all the little ones you skipped. Then take a magnifying glass to see how many you missed. You'll soon discover that the skin on your thumb has a lot of character you never knew about before.

The next time you are out on your favorite stream and you notice there is a hatch on, stop fishing, catch an insect and look at it as carefully as you examined your own thumb. I'll bet you a six-pack you'll see some things about that insect that you never would have dreamed possible. When that stark realization hits you, you are ready to tie some serious flies for some serious trout.

I'm not trying to say that you need to try to tie mayflies with eyeballs and kneecaps. You have to draw the line on detail someplace. What I am saying is that we need to learn to look at the insect and notice what we see, not what we have been told is there. Squint your eyelids so you will be looking through your eyelashes when you look at the insect you have just captured. The light rays reflected from the insect's body and wings will be refracted by your eyelashes in such a manner as to enhance the subtle shades of color, thereby making them clearer to you than before. If the mayfly you have captured is a late spring blue-winged olive, for example, you will probably notice that the abdomen is not just light green in color. In fact, it is probably creamy pale yellow, with bands of pale green the color of pea soup and highlighted with tints of light gray at the segment edges. If there is a lot of iron in the soil near your stream, you may notice slight hints of pale orange in the abdomen as well. Your dubbing mix should contain all the colors you see, because if you can see them, you can bet the trout can too. Perhaps the extra edge for fishing success on your stream is mixing and blending a dubbing mixture for specific hatches. How many times have you seen small packages of dubbing in your favorite fly shop that are labeled "Light Cahill," or "Blue-Winged Olive?" It must be the right stuff, because it was manufactured by a reputable company, right? Wrong. The underlying assumption is that *all* natural blue-winged olives are the same color. If you've been observant while you've been out fishing, you will have noticed that few colors of pre-packaged dubbing are the correct color. Close, but not entirely accurate, and you've lost an edge if you've used them.

The large trout in the popular, hard-fished streams act like they've seen it all before. Robert Traver stated so very clearly, "All men are equal before the trout." Why is it, then, that some men seem a little more equal than others? I think it's because some fishermen have developed a tiny extra edge, not only in their casting skills and approach to the trout, but in the equipment they choose as well. I'm not referring to the reel or the rod or the line. Though they are very important, their real function is as an extension of your arm to cast the leader and the fly to the fish. Well-designed leaders with long fine tippets are becoming more popular and seem to be more necessary as the trout are being herded around in our streams by more fly fishers who know how to cast with far greater skill than they know how to wade quietly. I've often wondered why it is that so many anglers spend so much money on, and pay so much attention to, the details on the wrong end of the fly line. If they took as much care in selecting or tying their flies as they did in the selection of the reel and rod, they might be able to gain the real extra edge that makes it possible to fool a fish that has, in fact, seen it all before.

It is with all the above in mind that I offer some ideas on fur color, and blending of fur for specific patterns. You need only a few items to create your own fur blends and, once again, you can find most of them at your local hardware store or fly shop. The most important piece of equipment is, of course, a good portable electric coffee grinder. Use it for mixing the colors by dropping a pinch of yellow and an equal pinch of white fur, for example, into the container where the blades are located. Put the top on the blender and alternately turn it on and off several times. (Several short bursts of power seem to mix the colors faster and more thoroughly than simply turning the blender on once and letting it run for several seconds.) It *is* possible to allow the blender to run too long; the blades inside are quite sharp and will gradually turn your dubbing fur into a fine dust if you're not careful. And don't ever attempt to remove the mixed dubbing until the rotating blades have completely stopped turning or you stand a good chance of painfully nicking a finger.

You will need some easily labeled containers to store your dubbing blends; I like those stacking, round plastic containers that screw together. Self-sticking labels adhere quite well to them. Bulk film cannisters of the type that 35mm film comes in work well for large amounts of dubbing such as hare's mask. Get to know a photographer at your hometown newspaper. They often buy their film in bulk cans and load their own film cartridges. If they don't get a credit for returning the containers to the film company, they probably throw them away. I have some old metal cans that I acquired years ago. I think they're made of plastic now, but they are still great containers for dubbing storage. The cans are round and about 1 1/2 inches high and four inches across. I don't like to use zip-lock

Fur blender, stacking cans, film cans

plastic bags because it always seems like the one I'm looking for is the one in the bottom of the drawer.

There are dozens of other containers that can be recycled for storage of your dubbing mixes. Your concern should be one of storage space for the containers and future availability.

The base colors I use for all my dubbing blends are: black, white, ginger, tan, brown, yellow, gray, olive, orange, and pink. I have found that by blending several of these colors together in varying proportions. I can very closely match almost all the colors I see in naturals. For dry flies I use rabbit with all the guard hairs removed and hare's mask (either dyed or natural) and, in some cases, hare's mask mixed with rabbit body including the guard hairs, for nymphs. I use some beaver to blend with rabbit for very tiny dry flies such as #20 and smaller *Baetis* duns. (See color plate #10, Base Colors, and #11, Dubbing Fur Blends.)

The enormous hole left in any discussion of color is that what I think of as olive and what you think of as olive may be vastly different. Even the finest photos often fail to accurately portray what the real colors of the subject are. When that failing is added to the photo reproduction in a book or magazine, where there is additional loss of color accuracy, the color that is seen by the reader and described as olive is now actually nothing more than a dark green. We can get very close, but we still need to catch the insects and take careful note of their colors as we compare them to our artificials.

I developed the following fur blends after hundreds of hours of studying natural insects and blending furs and colors in an attempt to match them as perfectly as possible. The proportions of "2 tan; 2 white; 1 yellow," for example, mean two parts (pinches) tan to two parts white and one part yellow. The amount of fur you determine to be a "pinch" is entirely up to you — just try to get an equal amount of fur for each pinch. The amount of fur you choose to call a pinch will also be determined to some extent by the capacity of your blender; too much fur will have a choking effect and the whirling blades won't be able to mix the fur. When blending fur for dry flies, remove all the guard hairs first and mix the fur in the blender to make a soft ball of dubbing. (Check Chapter 4 for some hints on removing guard hair.) There will no doubt be some geographic differences in the actual color of the insects in your area when compared to the recipe results given below. You'll have to make some minor adjustments. The following recipes are for some of the more important hatches. You'll no doubt come up with many more for your own needs. Make note of the proportions on a self-sticking label and attach it to the container in which you store the blend.

Each of the following blends is designed to be one shade lighter than the natural insect, as the material will darken when it gets wet or when you apply a water-proofing material such as silicone paste or liquid to the fly. Also, keep in mind that the underside of the insect is usually lighter in color than the back. Always attempt to match the belly color, not the back.

Slate-Winged Drake
2 tan
2 white
1 yellow

Light Hendrickson
1 tan
1 ginger
2 white
$\frac{1}{2}$ pink

Green Drake Emerger
3 olive
1 brown
$\frac{1}{2}$ gray

Colorado Green Drake
5 cream
1 olive
1 gray
$\frac{1}{2}$ yellow

Blue-Winged Olive
3 white
$\frac{1}{2}$ yellow
1 ginger
1 olive
$\frac{1}{2}$ gray

Baetis Dun
3 white
$\frac{1}{2}$ yellow
1 olive
1 gray

March Brown
1 cream
1 ginger
1 brown

Light Cahill
    2 white
    $^1/_2$ yellow
    $^1/_4$ tan

Olive Caddis Larva
    1 olive
    1 brown
    1 gray
    $^1/_4$ yellow

***Baetis* Nymph**
    1 olive
    $^1/_2$ cream
    1 gray
    $^1/_4$ yellow

Golden Stone Nymph
    1 yellow
    1 orange
    $^1/_2$ brown

Rusty Spinner
    2 tan
    1 orange
    1 yellow
    1 cream

Pale Morning Dun
    1 ginger
    1 cream
    $^1/_4$ yellow
    $^1/_2$ olive
    $^1/_4$ gray

Cinnamon Ant
> 1 tan
> $1/2$ orange
> $1/2$ cream

Pale Evening Dun
> 1 white
> $1/2$ yellow
> $1/4$ ginger

Olive Midge
> 1 yellow
> $1/4$ olive

Brown Stone Nymph
> 1 brown hare's mask
> 1 $1/2$ orange body fur

Dark Blue Dun
> 1 dark gray
> $1/2$ olive

To lighten the color of any dubbing blend listed above, add half a pinch of white or cream and blend. Repeat until you think it's right. To darken the color of any dubbing blend, add half a pinch of the darkest component in the recipe and blend, repeating until you're satisfied.

You may want to alter certain patterns or recipes by adding a little sparkle to the blend. I seldom do this, but when I do I use Aunt Lydia's Rug Yarn for the sparkle material. Cut about three inches of yarn into 1/4-inch lengths, drop a few in your blender and give it a few short bursts to create a small loose ball of sparkle fibers. (Don't allow the blender to run for more than just short bursts or the artificial fibers will heat up and turn into little balls of plastic.) I usually use an ivory or cream/white color for this purpose. It doesn't take much of this material to add noticeable sparkle to the finished fly. Add half a pinch at a time. Keep in mind that the sparkle material will make the fly body fuzzier than usual.

Cut rug yarn

Index